The Mantle of Fire

*God's Empowerment of the Joseph-Daniels
and God's Economy*

by

Morris E. Ruddick

Copyright © 2016 by Morris E. Ruddick

The Mantle of Fire
God's Empowerment of the Joseph-Daniels and God's Economy
by Morris E. Ruddick

Printed in the United States of America

ISBN 9781498460217

All rights reserved solely by the author. The author guarantees all contents are original and do not infringe upon the legal rights of any other person or work. No part of this book may be reproduced in any form without the permission of the author. The views expressed in this book are not necessarily those of the publisher.

Unless otherwise indicated, scripture quotations are taken from The New King James Version of the Bible. Copyright © 1979, 1980, 1982 by Thomas Nelson, Inc.

www.xulonpress.com

Paul,

Praise God for you and your very key role in this empowerment!

Yours in Jesus,

Maria

ALSO AVAILABLE
BY MORRIS RUDDICK

THE JOSEPH-DANIEL CALLING: Facilitating the Release of the Wealth of the Wicked

GOD'S ECONOMY, ISRAEL AND THE NATIONS: Discovering God's Ancient Kingdom Principles of Business and Wealth

THE HEART OF A KING: The Leadership Measure of the Joseph-Daniel Calling

SOMETHING MORE: A Devotional Dimension for the Joseph-Daniel Calling

RIGHTEOUS POWER IN A CORRUPT WORLD: The Application of God's Leadership Strategy

LEADERSHIP BY ANOINTING: The Jewish Strategy and Biblical Model for Leadership

TABLE OF CONTENTS

DEDICATION

G od mobilized my wife and I as committed Christians during the early days of the charismatic revival. These were days in which the atmosphere was electric with God. The dynamic we refer to as revival was manifesting everywhere. Almost everyone we knew was affected.

It was a time when the conscious presence of the Lord was being evidenced in neighborhoods and workplaces. There was a hunger for God that caused people from wide varieties of theological persuasions to get together to pray and seek God. Something very pure and very real was happening. The result was expectations being exceeded for those who responded.

Now, a generation later, what we witnessed in those days is manifesting again. However, it carries new dimensions. It is manifesting strongly in the marketplace and in some of the most unlikely places. It also dovetails with the rebirth of Israel and ancient mysteries tied to the restoration of God's order and covenant promises made long ago.

Participating in some of these more recent developments, my wife and I have had the opportunity to spend extended periods of time working closely with the brethren in Vietnam. Vietnam is one of those places in the world where becoming a believer costs. My closest working associate there spent almost three years in a hard-labor prison for his faith. Many risk their lives in their quest for religious freedom.

Today, most Christians in Vietnam still live under varying degrees of restraint and persecution. Despite that, the believers in this land are on the cusp of revival. They are gripped with God's priorities and the restoration of Israel. It is singularly one of the most diligent segments of the church globally in terms of their fervency in prayer.

Today, the dedication and leadership found in this emerging nation and others like it are starting to manifest within a prepared remnant of the marketplace globally. These are the modern-day Josephs and Daniels.

Together with those emerging from the fires of persecution, they are the ones who will bear mantles of fire.

This book is dedicated to those we have been honored to serve alongside in Vietnam and other regions of the world, whose hunger for more of God knows no restraint. It is dedicated to those members of the Body who have paid high costs and not wavered in their zeal for more of God. It is dedicated to those who will not be satisfied with the status quo and who yearn to see His glory manifested. It is dedicated to the prepared remnant of Josephs and Daniels of this day. Together, these are the forerunners wielding the mantle of fire. These are the ones paving the way for the restoration that will trigger the operation of God's economy during a time of great turbulence and reversals. My prayer in dedicating this book targets those with this insatiable hunger for more of God. I pray each will be filled beyond their expectations. I pray not one would be disappointed.

ACKNOWLEDGEMENTS

For their insightful and valued review of this manuscript, together with the impartation of a wisdom that has been in keeping with the strategic nature of this effort, I want to express my deepest appreciation to Steve Martin and Dan Collier.

I similarly am very indebted to those dear friends who have faithfully stood in the gap and upheld us with their prayers, as we have reached for more of the Lord. My gratefulness for the sacrifice and significant value of these sustaining prayers far exceeds what words might try to express.

PREFACE

THE MANDATE
FOR THE MANTLE

T he setting was pretty grim. Having been at the helm of orchestrating a major, successful corporate turnaround, I found myself a casualty of some unscrupulous, behind-the-scenes corporate politics. In my attempt to understand what had happened spiritually, I simply asked the Lord why it seemed the harder I tried to be obedient in following Him, the more I seemed to experience the bottom dropping out. This wasn't the first instance of something collapsing that I knew had been ordered by the Lord.

Without hesitation, the answer the Lord gave me was that it was because of the calling on my life. Specifically, He explained that I was called to an arena in which secular enterprises would be linked together with objectives that would serve His Kingdom.

The time was the mid-1980s. Having walked with the Lord since the early 70s, I still seemed to be grasping at straws in understanding the unorthodox calling on my life.

A Company of Josephs

My calling and the calling of a global company of others is one patterned after the Patriarch Joseph. Little did I realize the significance of the change that would surround the unfolding of this twenty-first century mantle. Nor at the time did I have a clue how this calling would accompany the restoration of the principles and ancient secrets the Lord has been imparting to his people from the days of Abraham.

It is a mantle of fire, one in which those so anointed and called have been prepared with great authority to bring change.

The calling of Joseph was distinctive. With clarity, he heard from the Lord with a keen understanding of God's heart and attentively acted on it. Joseph broke ranks with religious traditions in his response to the voice of God.

In giving testimony to his prophetic dreams, he found life as he had known it taking an abrupt turn, as he lost his freedom, his family and any semblance of status and power.

Joseph was suddenly immersed in the world's system in a distant culture. His response was to adapt to being an incomparable prophetic steward with both the mundane and as God's emissary. His unequivocal identity in God combined with the Lord being the source of his exploits, as God's hand upon him was made obvious to all.

"The Lord was with Joseph and he was a successful man and everyone saw that the Lord was with Joseph and made all that he did to prosper." Genesis 39:2-3

Joseph mastered his new culture from the bottom-up before being entrusted with the resources and future of the nation. Then his efforts in the amassing of grain became not just the means to feed the people, but served as the commodity of value when the money failed. All this was a backdrop to restoring and protecting God's people from the judgment encroached at their door.

Exhibiting prudent discipline, Joseph's stewardship anticipated opportunity for the common good. He cornered the livestock market and later took over the land, until when the famine passed he eventually turned the land back to its owners in a modified land-grant program.

Joseph oversaw the greatest wealth transfer the world had ever known.

Unorthodox Change

Apart from a prudent, self-sustaining means for his family to care for themselves in Goshen, not one religious program is mentioned in his activities other than his unswerving commitment to and identity in God – and Joseph acting on the prophetic insights he received from the Lord.

Yet no hero of faith achieved greater exploits for God in the context of harnessing the world's system than did Joseph.

He clearly linked secular enterprises and resources to establish a Kingdom model designed for the care and redemption of God's people as he gained the trust and allied with the source of these resources during times of great challenge and change.

In so doing he demonstrated the sovereignty of God over both the secular and those called by His name. Operating under great prophetic authority, he provided a safe place for ALL those under his authority

Understanding the Times

Understanding this mantle begins with an understanding of the times from a big-picture, God-perspective. Isaiah 60 tells of a time when darkness will cover the earth and deep darkness the people.

Today we are on the threshold of such a time. Isaiah 60 prophetically paints a portrait of a time in which God is restoring His order to His creation and preparing to fulfill the promises to His people that began with His covenant with Abraham.

"Darkness shall cover the earth, and deep darkness the people. But the LORD will arise over you and His glory will be seen upon you. The Gentiles shall come to your light and kings to the brightness of your rising. Isaiah 60:2-3

The focal point is Israel.

A Shift of Power and Resources

Isaiah went on to prophesy (Isa 60:8) that the abundance of the sea would be directed to Israel and the wealth of the nations would come to them. The ramp-up of turbulence and lawlessness underway today is related. It represents the periphery of the birth pangs spoken of by Jesus in Matthew 24 and Mark 13. It portends a time of great restoration, a vast shift of wealth and power. Bringing change during this time will require the mantle of fire.

For the sake of the zealots and prematurely eager – and not in any way to dampen the intentions of those genuinely called, it should be remembered that the calling of Joseph involved serious betrayal by those closest to him, along with a complete loss of his status and freedom. It involved an extremely long waiting period for God's set time, a wait involving some very humble conditions.

Yet, during his wait even as a slave, Joseph exemplified the mantle of his great-grandfather Abraham, whose calling was to be blessed to be a blessing. The wealth transfer will be stewarded by those who not only have paid the cost of the calling, but have been uniquely prepared.

These will be men and women of God whose prophetic gift and authority, sensitivity to God's heart and stellar obedience to His guidance marks their identity and wisdom to those in non-religious circles. They are people of trust who worldly power brokers will seek to align themselves with.

The calling will functionally be diverse. From a human standpoint it will involve an element of compartmentalized enterprises, reflecting numerous divinely-connected, yet self- and mutually-supporting enterprises.

The Joseph calling is at the crux of this great time of restoration, of this shift of power and wealth.

The Issues from God's Perspective

To better understand this shift of power and wealth requires a look at three key spheres of influence: culture, economic and power.

The Culture. Culturally, this great shift will divide the sheep from the goats. It will exhibit a sweeping spiritual awakening accompanied by great signs and wonders. This spiritual awakening will be paralleled with the fires of unprecedented persecution. Despite that, this time will reflect innovative alliances between secular institutions that fulfill overriding self-sustaining Kingdom purposes.

The way of the Kingdom will define both the identity and culture of true believers. The Kingdom model is comprehensive in combining the spiritual, entrepreneurial and community, a model familiar to those in touch with the Hebraic roots of the faith.

The result will reorder foundations of culture, power and the economic. The Josephs now coming into position are forerunners in what is now being termed the marketplace movement. It is the restoration of societal-spiritual leadership that interlinks the Kingdom with the secular, business with ministry, if you will.

God's Economy. A study in *Global Inc*. (Gabel, Bruner, 2003, New York), notes that 53 of the world's 100 largest economies are corporations. That's a major twist in outlook. Despite the change that can be expected in the days ahead, in the same way that God sent Joseph to prepare Egypt as a safe place, preparations are already underway globally for the shift that lies before us.

God has been preparing both select corporations and nation-states as safe-places and Kingdom harbingers. With modern-day Josephs in key roles, they will become hubs of extraordinary alliances of secular enterprises serving Kingdom objectives. They will be self-supporting models, prepared and ahead of the power curve of the amassing global turbulence.

With unique ties to Israel, there will be a keen focus on new discoveries, inventions and advanced technologies that serve the purpose of averting and navigating the chaos, disasters and persecution in establishing the foundations in which God dwells with His people.

Kingdom Power. Revival attracts. The global spiritual awakening, demonstrating God's power and restoring ancient truths of the faith beginning with God's covenant with Abraham will sweep every sector of society.

Leadership will accompany the anointing of those who unwaveringly have paid the cost, like Joseph in having lost everything personally meaningful. They will be ones who within their spheres are graced with unusual trust and favor, but also are targets, initially even with their brethren.

The Book of Revelation describes a time of varying discord and hostility against believers. Those leading the way through the persecution will be those who already bear the brand-marks of the Lord Jesus (2 Cor 11:23).

In this last generation, starting with the Cultural Revolution, key segments of the church in Asia have gone through a cleansing of its Western trappings and accoutrements. Those who withstood and survived this and other similar purges became a pure church, one with a very humble dependency based solely on God and a genuine prayer-base. From this foundation, God's power was released in a manner closely resembling the early church.

A Time of Restoration

The release of Kingdom power will bring restoration of the ancient paths. The restoration will trigger a process. At the core will be Israel. At the climax will be the fulfillment of the Kingdom and every promise uttered by God to His covenant people.

In the process of God's restoration of Israel, emphasis will be given to inventions, technologies and potential discoveries that build the foundations for Israel and God's Kingdom intentions. Accompanying investments and alliances will engender Israel's means of being self-sustaining. The strategic agendas will range from the return of the House of Israel to the land, to mechanisms that enhance the role of genuine friends of Israel (John 15:13-14), to initiatives toward Israel's energy independence, to advanced technologies, to discoveries that bring healing and fertility to the nations.

The Sound of the Kingdom

"Holy, holy, holy is the Lord of Hosts. The whole earth is filled with His glory."
Isaiah 6:3

The sound of the Kingdom will conform to the patterns and responses exhibited by Jesus in His earthly ministry. His unveiling of the Kingdom released the harmony by which the natural and the spiritual realms are bridged.

The sound of the Kingdom will be accompanied by the mantle of fire. The mantle of fire is the empowerment of the marketplace emissaries paving this new ground of restoration. Those anointed with this mantle will be found operating with a power beyond the realm of human effort. John's gospel progressively disclosed the simple secret of power that Jesus imparted to His followers: God-in-us and the dynamic of abiding in Him.

This power and the mantle of fire involve the simple things that confound the wise. It releases God's most unlikely candidates executing the most unlikely strategies to bring about the most unlikely results.

Put simply, the players and strategies ahead will not conform to the way people normally view religious things. Jesus pointed to the Father being in Him and Jesus being in the Father (John 14:10-11). John quoted Jesus as saying: "On that day you will know that I am in My Father and you in Me, and I in you." (John 14:19-21) The issue is God dwelling with and manifesting Himself through His covenant people.

That is why the marketplace movement is so significant. THAT also is how you distinguish Joseph from his brothers. Pharaoh saw it clearly and stated: "Can we find such a one as this, a man in whom is the Spirit of God?" (Gen 41:38)

Just as Joseph served God's purposes in Egypt, today's Josephs are God's advance party. Their apostolic-prophetic role in some very chaotic conditions will be served in very practical terms, in strategies that link secular enterprises with overriding ministry objectives in restoring God's order.

Today's Josephs are the forerunners, the servant-leaders, heeding the sound of the Kingdom, wielding the mantle of fire, serving as the foundation of the apostles and prophets for the restoration of the ancient purposes being triggered by the anointed description captured by the Apostle Paul.

"God's household, having been built upon the foundation of the apostles and prophets, Jesus Himself being the cornerstone, is now being built into a holy temple of the Lord in whom you also are being fitted together as a dwelling for God in the Spirit." Ephesians 2:19-22

SECTION I

THE DYNAMIC

CHAPTER 1

THE MANTLE OF FIRE

"If you walk in my ways and perform my service, then you will be given authority over my House. I will let you walk in and out of my presence along with these others standing here." Zechariah 3:7 NASU and NLT

A gain and again, the Word of God describes the Lord's presence and glory as a consuming fire. From Exodus, Deuteronomy, Isaiah to Hebrews, the awesome essence of the Lord's holiness is revealed in this manner.

Throughout the Word of God are instances in which individuals have been consumed by the fire of His presence. Isaiah describes the response of the unrighteous to His presence simply as being terrifying.

"The sinners in Zion are terrified; trembling grips the godless. For who can dwell with the consuming fire?" Isaiah 33:14 NIV

There are also cases in which the Lord has made allowance by covering chosen ones with the shadow of His hand. Scripture then unveils a time of salvation, when supernaturally, God Himself will intervene to present the prophets, the saints and all who fear His Name, as faultless before the presence of His glory. (Jude 1:24-25 and Rev 11:18)

In moving toward that time, we recognize if only by a glimmer, a role of the chosen in this pathway of walking with Him. It is a role marked by holiness, as described in the opening passage from Zechariah. It reveals those who are given authority, a mantle of fire, drawn from broaching the gates and accessing His presence.

The Turmoil and the Expectation

With the heightened level of confusion and disorder in today's world, it is essential to stay focused on what God is doing. God is restoring His order to His creation. We are marching toward the fulfillment of restoration described in Isaiah 60, which points to the rebuilding of the broken walls of prophetic destiny designed for God's covenant people.

The mantle of fire marks the anointing of those who usher in agendas that fulfill key prophecies and the release of accompanying moves of His Spirit.

Once again, not unlike the days described by Acts 15, God is restoring the tabernacle of David. In the same way that this bore great significance for the early Church, so it will be the catalyst for the greatest move of God this generation has ever seen.

"With this the words of the prophets agree, as it is written: 'After this I will return and will rebuild the tabernacle of David, which has fallen down; I will rebuild its ruins, and I will restore it; so the rest of mankind may seek the Lord, even all the Gentiles who are called by My name, says the Lord who does all these things.'" Acts 15:15-17

When God is sovereignly moving, "more of the same harder" will run into a ditch. It is a time to hold steady and move with faithful caution. Being alert and prepared incorporates the need to understand what is to be expected.

Embracing the New Thing. It is a time to look sharply to discern what has been embraced as truth, but in reality falls into the realm of the precepts of men. The times call for careful search of the ancient paths to discern and embrace the dimensions to be restored. This restoration will be as a new thing to our generation.

This new thing God is doing and the authority for the mantle of fire are tied to His holiness and power. It will be marked by the restoration of many ancient mysteries.

"Thus says the Lord: Stand at the crossroads and look. Then ask for the ancient paths where the good way lies. Then walk in it and you will find rest for your souls." Jeremiah 6:16

Being alert to the new and restored dimensions of what God is doing may stretch us beyond our comfort zones and require a fresh alignment of our hearts with His. Such an alignment is predicated on seeking Him with a pure and unencumbered heart.

Acting on Unusual Prophetic Authority. The clash in the spiritual climates taking place around us will trigger the release of unusual prophetic authority and the mantle to open gates. These are gates of opportunity for change aligned with God's purposes. These alignments will often be accompanied by miraculous signs not unlike the time Elijah called down the fire to break the grip that evil had over God's people.

Recognizing the Alliances between Jews and Gentiles. The mantle of fire will result in unexpected alliances between committed believers and Bible-believing Jews.

The latter-day restoration of the tabernacle of David will trigger the spark for manifesting great waves of God's glory.

Enmities held for generations will dissolve and manifest in supernatural, biblically cooperative alliances between the most unlikely. Isaiah prophesied that jealousy, enmity and hostility generated by Ephraim (Hos 9:8) would end, giving rise to a coming together, a unity that would overcome the forces long being arrayed against Judah.

"Yet the Lord will lift up a standard for the nations, and assemble the banished ones of Israel, and gather the dispersed of Judah from the corners of the earth. Then the jealousy of Ephraim will depart, and those who harass Judah will be cut off." Isaiah 11:12-13

Maintaining the Momentum. Between the turmoil and what God is releasing will be events that transpire quickly. The potential to be overwhelmed must be resisted by a fervent focus to giving priority to time seeking the Lord. Whatever sphere of influence we walk into we should immediately begin looking beyond it, lest it overwhelm us.

Having appeared to Moses in a burning bush, God's awesome, holy, manifested presence has a long history of providing strategic direction and changing the course of things. From the pillar of fire by night to the demonstration of the tongues of fire with the outpouring of the Spirit on the day of Pentecost; the demonstration of fire has punctuated His power accompanying a holy and pure mantle.

God's glory, operating through Moses, led the children of Israel out of bondage and into the threshold of the Promised Land. So the awesome manifestation of His presence will move God's modern-day, sold-out remnant, appointed and anointed, walking in repentance and consecration, into times that will see an application of His power that will exceed that of the Book of Acts.

Stewarding the Mantle of Fire

The mantle of fire incorporates the stewardship of power.

Two of the three temptations the devil brought to Jesus involved the profane, misuse of power: *"Command that these stones be made bread"* and *"throw yourself down, for it is written 'He will give His angels charge over you.'"* The third involved the enticement of corrupt power: *"All these things I will give to you."*

Each of these temptations was a sacrilegious, unauthorized means to replicate and bypass the power that comes from God's glory. They represented myopic, religious defilements of God's power and counterfeits of both the glory and the blessing. In the time before us, the enticements and the evil use of power will abound.

God's antidote is the mantle of fire which employs only a pure holy fire.

"He who speaks from himself seeks his own glory; but He who is seeking the glory of the One who sent Him, He is true, and there is no unrighteousness in Him." John 7:18

Before becoming the pure sacrifice that would bring fulfillment to what was outlined by the law and the prophets, Jesus gave his followers the sacrament of the Lord's Supper. The Lord's Supper, referred to by some as communion, is a significant New Covenant practice paralleling the Leviticus 9 process to actuate the glory that releases the blessing and power of God.

The Pure Mantle of the Fire of Glory and Power

Jesus warned of strange fire through the parable of the tares. When attempting to mix the impure with the pure, it backfires.

Pure fire is the most potent catalyst to the release of the blessing and power of God. It is also the most powerful response to encounters with aggressive strongholds, and actuates the release of judgment.

"If you have run with footmen and they have wearied you, then how will you contend with horses? If in the land of peace in which you trusted, they wearied you then how will you do in the floodplain of the Jordan?" Jeremiah 12:5

However, strange fire results when the pure process is modified or defiled with a replacement.

Strange fire and replacement of the purity of God's process has been at the core of the enemy's strategy from the beginning. The pure was defiled by eating the forbidden fruit in the garden. Similarly, the pure process was corrupted by the sons of Aaron, just as the profane was added by Ananias and Sapphira. The defilement of the pure was reflected by the Hellenization of the Gospel, the expungement of the Jewish roots to the faith in the time of Constantine; and in each instance whereby the precepts of men employed the seductive use of strange fire that impeded entrance within the veil. It is within the veil that the pure fire is released.

The times demand not just the pure fire, but the restoration of the holy process without the polluted add-ons. Daniel noted that in the time of the end many would be purified and refined, but that wickedness would increase and abound. The times upon us are bordering between the times of sorrow spoken of by Jesus in Matthew 24 and the times of the end described by Daniel. Wickedness is on the increase and gaining root.

A recent dream received by a respected ministry associate of ours showed three gargoyles: one with its hands over its ears, another with its hands over its eyes and the third with its hands over its mouth. From the pit has been released an assault of spiritual deafness, spiritual blindness and a perversion of spiritual authority.

High-level religious spirits wielding deception and confusion have been planting disorder and division (James 3:16) among the very elect. The cleverness of the clever will fall short. It is the time Jesus described (Matt 24) in which *"many will be offended and betray one another; false prophets will arise and deceive many; and because lawlessness will abound, the love of many will grow cold."*

The Unstoppable Dynamic

The early church was seen by the world as *"those who are turning the world upside down."* Their faith-response involved sacrifice and, as a people, THEY became the catalysts to releasing the Glory and Power. There's nothing to compare with that complete exchange of His life for ours, within community, to actuate the maturity spoken of by Paul to the Ephesians.

True spiritual maturity leads. It is evidenced by those who take responsibility beyond their selves, face the fire, and penetrate the veil to reverse the bondages. The full knowledge of the Lord (Eph 4) is not a head-thing or the resolution of all our soulish issues; but rather an operational application of the mantle of fire.

That doesn't come from a Sunday-go-to-meeting, adapted to-the-world orientation. It demands a pure Kingdom mind-set and identity; by which we live by dying, our weaknesses become the seedbed for His strength, we advance by yielding and lead by serving, we bless our enemies, wisdom comes from simplicity, our purpose in life comes from giving it up, honor flows from humility and growth results from proactive generosity. Jesus raised the bar.

We are in a time in which the wisdom and power that flowed in the early church is not just being restored. It will become the launch-pad for even greater levels of the release of His power and glory.

Those wielding the mantle of pure fire will pierce the extremes of darkness with God's glory and power. The pure fire has always been tied to God's presence and the consumption of darkness in its wake. The word to the church for this day is to reach for the fire, the pure fire.

"I will establish them and multiply them, and I will set My sanctuary in their midst. My tabernacle also shall be with them; indeed I will be their God, and they shall be My people. Then the nations will know that I, the LORD, sanctify Israel, when My sanctuary is in their midst." Ezekiel 37:26-28

CHAPTER 2

SHARED ANOINTINGS

"Elijah said to Elisha, 'Ask! What may I do for you, before I am taken away from you?' Elisha said, 'Please let a double portion of your spirit be upon me.'" 2 Kings 2:9

Elijah's God-encounter in the cave which followed his exploits against the prophets of Baal and Asherah began a transition for Elijah's ministry, as well as for Israel. After challenging Elijah's hideaway with the words: "What are you doing here;" the Lord then restored him to fulfill his next task. Soon afterward, Elijah was connected with Elisha as his protégé and the process of Elisha's nurturing began. (1 Kings 19:16).

The authority of Elijah's anointing shut up the heavens and brought judgment on a reprobate Israel. Then his daring confrontation with evil changed Israel's spiritual climate. In so doing, God's people began coming out of the closet.

So when Elisha asked for a double portion of Elijah's spirit, it was no small thing. Elijah bore a disruptive anointing; an anointing that short-circuited the inroads of evil. His authority in the spirit stopped sorcery in its tracks. It had no equal in that day.

The fulfillment of Elisha's request for a "double-portion" was evidenced not only by the startling miracles of his ministry, but by the angelic host unveiled around him in his encounter with the army of Syria (2 Kings 6:17). 2 Kings 13:21 then tells of a burial interrupted by a band of raiders. The dead man was abandoned in the tomb of Elisha and Scripture indicates that when "he was let down and touched the bones of Elisha, he revived and stood on his feet." So Elisha's double-portion of Elijah's anointing not only worked unusual miracles, it commanded the authority of a host of angels and carried a presence that even transcended his death.

God's highest priorities are always about His people. For both Elijah and Elisha, their greatest accomplishments involved the impact on the spiritual climate to mobilize God's people and impart the prophetic wisdom as advisors to protect those known by His Name.

These dynamics raise two very important issues. First is what Elisha reached for: a dimension in God beyond the incredible spiritual threshold that operated through his mentor. The second is the issue of the anointing itself, and with the anointing the authority, available for the challenges within the church of this day.

The release of the anointing comes at a cost. It involves a stewardship. The stewardship is in the reach one makes for God's presence; which in turn abides in the place of His glory. The operation of the anointing requires a God-perspective, which means adjusting our mind-sets, to thinking according to God's order and standard. The release of the anointing manifests when operating in the Spirit beyond one's human capacities. Shared anointings come from mentoring and cooperative assignments directed by the Spirit for the purpose of the community at large.

Operation of the Anointing

Jesus taught his followers how to apply righteous power in corrupt settings. This is the way of the Kingdom. It begins with our thinking.

"Let this mind be in you which also was in Christ Jesus." Philippians 2:5

The anointing flows when there is not one vestige of variation between God's order and purposes; and our actions and words. It is an emptying of ourselves in humility to allow the unhindered flow of the Holy Spirit through us.

"Who emptied Himself, taking on the form of a bondservant." Philippians 2:7

Jesus taught His followers to abide. Jesus spent hours at night in prayer with the Father. He imparted the wisdom that He always did what He saw His father doing.

"I am the vine, you are the branches; he who abides in Me, and I in him, he bears much fruit; for apart from Me you can do nothing." John 15:5-6

Upon His resurrection, a new thing happened. Jesus made the Holy Spirit available to all believers (John 14:26-27). The ongoing release of the Spirit follows the pattern of Jesus in spending time with the Father and abiding. Many were those who followed after Elijah, but only Elisha stayed the course to embrace the "double-portion."

The Release of the Anointing

The anointing serves as a catalyst, an igniter of righteous power. Abiding in the place of His presence, the place of His glory penetrates the veil. It is the place where the supernatural power of God to trump evil is revealed.

Yet the anointing is released when what we see in the Spirit-realm is put into action. From his place of abiding Elisha discerned the very words the King of Syria spoke in the privacy of his bedchamber. From that he advised the King of Israel. So in 2 Kings 6 when the armies of Syria came by night and surrounded Elisha's city, he knew exactly what was unfolding and he knew what he was to do.

Joseph the Patriarch, a slave without position, brought blessing to the household of Potiphar. Genesis 39 indicates that everyone saw that the Lord was with Joseph and made all that he did to prosper. Joseph knew what it meant to abide in God's presence, but as a faithful steward Joseph put in action what God showed him. He carried the mantle of his great-grandfather Abraham, as a catalyst of blessing to those around him, indeed to the nations.

Shared Anointings

Individual anointings are multiplied exponentially when combined and released with the anointings of others. The scope of Elisha's mantle expanded as Elijah mentored, nurtured and prepared him. It is the reason why biblical community represents a safe-place to foster the diversity of gifts and anointings; where they are allowed to incubate and work together. However, since Jesus' resurrection and the outpouring of the Holy Spirit, shared anointings have taken on an even greater potential.

The charismatic revival of the late sixties and early seventies began when believers hungry for more of God, began gathering to seek Him more diligently. What resulted was shared and passed on by the laying on of hands. Ripples went out that became a torrent of revival as the anointing was imparted and the presence of God manifested to satisfy the growing hunger of those not satisfied with the status quo.

Over the years, within my calling in the marketplace, I have been given opportunity to apply my gift and impart my anointing as a consultant to a number of respected ministries, ranging from CBN to Oral Roberts, to Morris Cerullo to Marilyn Hickey. In each of these cases not only did result come from the application of my gift; but I emerged with a dimension of the anointing from these ministries I had served.

When anointings merge to serve God's purposes, new dimensions are released on each side.

Many years ago, I received a prophetic word from a minister I had never met before who had no awareness of my situation or background. His words to me simply were: "You sir, have a spirit of prosperity on you. Financially, you may be broke or you may be a millionaire. It doesn't matter. Prosperity is not about money; but comes from within to bring blessing and increase to others." That word came not long after I had lost my position with a firm I had been working for. My financial situation at the time was not good.

Yet, the words of truth this man of God spoke penetrated the darkness trying to enshroud me at that time. It bore significantly on assignments I had had in the past bearing on opportunity and increase for my clients; as it has become foundational to the role I now serve with the persecuted church within God's purposes in making them the head and not the tail.

Yet, what has resulted, as a consultant, a board-member and a teacher-mobilizer comes from shared anointings, which combine the dimensions of my own anointing being blended with the unique dimensions of those I have served and am serving.

As a young Christian, I was greatly influenced and mentored by two incredible men of God. Both might be described as world-class prayer warriors; men of faith. Yet one also had a unique anointing for developing strategy; while the other's distinctive anointing was tied to being a catalyst for revival. Now, since that time in the early seventies, prayer, developing strategy and revival are still by-words of the way my anointing operates.

The more you impart to apply and give your anointing away, the more it grows. It is a dynamic of the Kingdom.

The Cost and Application

The issue comes down to two factors. The first is the cost of the anointing. The second is in applying the anointing. The anointing of an Elijah or Elisha does not come passively. It is developed and nurtured. It flows with one's gifts and calling.

Every believer has a sphere (2 Cor 10:13), an area of influence of their anointing. Within the boundary of that area of influence is the authority to break asunder what Paul refers to as the bondage of corruption. Presumption in operating outside that sphere is asking for trouble. The bottom line is in changing the spiritual climate.

Daniel excelled professionally and spiritually in a culture of sorcery to the level that he was described as ten times better than ALL the sorcerers within the king's realm. From that juncture and standard, there came stages of challenge: the king's dream; walking in the fire; and the lion's den. Changing the spiritual climate will not generally go unchallenged. However, there comes a point in prevailing when one's spiritual authority becomes established.

So it was, later in Daniel's tenure as advisor to the court. It was in that context that the handwriting on the wall manifested. It was a major shift from the lion's den and walking in the fire. The handwriting on the wall parallels Joseph's promotion alongside Pharaoh, when the anointing prevails and has established God's authority in a domain. When it does, everything changes.

Yet, the mantle bearing the anointing requires a cost. Many years ago, a great man of God I studied under told the story of a young man who came to him and audaciously told him he "wanted" his anointing. Very few in that generation had an anointing to equal the authority this man of God wielded. His response to the young man very simply was: "Are you willing to pay the cost?"

We impart and share the anointing generously. However, to fully embrace the anointing of others, a cost will be paid.

Sometimes the cost already has been paid at the point of impartation and reflects a "next step" for what the Lord has planned. That very much has been the case with the persecuted segment of the church we have been honored to be working with. They have been through and have been purified by fire. Elisha had been prepared by the best and was ready for the double-portion.

Yet for others, the impartation will result in having to face and then walk into the fire. It has never been about man's glory, but God's; and His alone. God is a consuming fire. His presence does not "abide" with the soulish. It disrupts and then consumes it.

God's anointing applied will bring change and the restoration of the order required to establish His purposes. The key for the Elijah-Elisha impact, the "double-portion" in today's time of turbulence, is to be found in exercising the anointing through community.

We need the authority of Elijah's anointing to shut up the heavens and bring judgment. We need God's people to come out of the closet. We need those who are either aligned with or overwhelmed by the world to arise and take their place among the remnant of the faithful, who have been applying their anointings.

It is time for the spiritual climate to be challenged with the explosive power of shared anointings from God's chosen.

The release of the anointing involves stewardship. Shared anointings ignite one another and bring enlargement. This type of prophetic stewardship requires a consistent priority of spending time with Him so that our perspective is a God-perspective. It means defining our gifts and like Daniel, becoming the best in the sphere we've been given. That means operating in the Spirit beyond our human capacities.

Entering this dimension requires focus given to mentoring and cooperative assignments directed by the Spirit that provide opportunity for shared anointings to manifest at the community level. This premise will evoke what will manifest as revival, as the fullness of His presence takes root.

"I will make them and the places around My hill a blessing. And I will cause showers to come down in their season; they will be showers of blessing. Also the tree of the field will yield its fruit and the earth will yield its increase, and they will be secure on their land. Then they will know that I am the LORD." Ezekiel 34:26-27

CHAPTER 3

THE REVIVAL CODE

"Bear one another's burdens and so fulfill the law of Christ." Galatians 6:2

I have heard many, who experienced the days of the charismatic revival, to describe it with the words: "It was like there was something in the air." Indeed there was. God was moving. There prevailed an awareness and expectation with God that simply incited a priority to being a part of it.

An author named Doug Wead ("Tonight They'll Kill a Catholic," Creation House, 1974) conducted research in war-torn Northern Ireland, during a time in which Protestants and Catholics were meeting together for prayer. His research was to verify the stories of incredible miracles that were coming from these gatherings. His observation was that in seven out of ten of the stories, there indeed had been amazing things that had happened, but the stories had been exaggerated. However, he noted that in three out of ten of the cases, that they could only be described with the word: "WOW!!"

That was a generation ago. Since that time, the Body of Christ has experienced much growth, both in numbers and maturity. Today when the word revival is raised, those with whom we are in close relationship, to a person, can be quoted as expressing a longing for more, much more of this dimension of God being at the forefront of everyday life.

Under the pressures of the Cultural Revolution, the church in China equally had spectacular growth and amazing stories of miracles. Church growth in places like Indonesia and Korea can be explained by nothing short of revival fires being released. Similarly, the church in Vietnam has emerged as a vibrant, praying church that has truly touched the hem of His garment.

The Issues

Yet, in defining sovereign moves of the Spirit, the question must be asked: What is it that distinguishes true revival from the contagion of a well-orchestrated program? From models of revival, what are the codes and strategies that ignite and sustain it? Likewise, is revival something that has manifested just since the Acts 2 outpouring of the Holy Spirit or is there precedent historically within the Jewish roots to the faith?

One of my favorite remembrances from the early 1970s, days of vibrant revival fires, was what we referred to as body ministry. It was one of the distinguishing characteristics of those days. Praying for one another was more spontaneous. We took time to gather; to bear one another's burdens.

I recall vividly small group gatherings that nurtured short words of wisdom, exhortations, testimonies of answered prayer, simple scriptures participants may have had on their hearts; all of which came together prophetically under the Spirit's guidance to form a theme that highlighted the time together and encouraged those who had gathered.

These interactive dynamics would be followed by spontaneous prayer as members of the group revealed needs tied to the words given. Spontaneity, Word-based, Spirit-led were the key factors that marked these gatherings. It was gatherings like this that became the spark that ignited revival in a broad, cross-section of the church.

Similarly, Acts 2 notes that the believers in the early church met daily and broke bread together in their homes; in addition to meeting in the temple. The Amplified version notes those gatherings included the Lord's Supper and prayers (v. 42). Paul gave instruction for such gatherings (1 Cor 14:26) with the admonition that when they came together that opportunity should be given for ministering to one another; building one another up. He made it clear that this vital function should be done under the guidance of leadership, decently and in order.

The Old Covenant is rich with historical references to what happened when God's people came together, as one. This was the purpose of the feast days which served purposes such as community-wide repentance (Yom Kippur), to celebrating God's deliverance of His people (Passover; the exact time paralleling Jesus' resurrection), to giving honor to Pentecost (the giving of God's Torah/Truth; which also was when the Acts 2 out-pouring of the Spirit happened).

"Now when Solomon had finished praying, fire came down from heaven and consumed the burnt offering and the sacrifices, and the glory of the LORD filled the house. The priests could not enter into the house of

the LORD because the glory of the LORD filled the LORD'S house." 2
Chronicles 7:1-3

Some of these community-wide gatherings involve fasting, but each
result in rejoicing, prayer and celebrating the Lord, which includes spiritually festive times of eating together.

"So you will sing as on the night you celebrate a holy festival; your hearts
will rejoice as when people go to the mountain of the Lord. The Lord will
cause men to hear his majestic voice and will make them see his anger and
consuming fire, with cloudburst, thunderstorm and hail. The voice of the
Lord will shatter His enemies; with his scepter he will strike them down."
Isaiah 30:29-31

The Dynamics
When revival is in evidence its prime dynamics will include the broad
community-response of believers; the priority given to God and His presence; and of hearing from Him; all of which engenders radical obedience
to God's standard and heart.

Community-Response. Revival fires that are unleashed at the community-
level will have an impact that affects the extended community: a broad
cross-section of churched and unchurched alike. It brings an insatiable
hunger for God as people reach out for the reality of God operating in
their midst.

It operates beyond denominational and doctrinal boundaries, while
adhering to central biblical common ground shared by all. Our pastor from
the early 70s once told us: "In our faith are matters for which we should
be willing to die. Those are the areas the Body needs to agree on." Revival
flows from those areas.

God's Presence and Priority. Times of revival are marked by the consciousness of God's presence and powerful answers to prayer. With a keen
focus on prayer, worship and seeking God, there is a reverence and cen-
trality to giving the priority necessary to take that "next step" with God.

It provokes a trust and spontaneity of gathering with those of a kindred
spirit to seek Him, in waiting on Him with prayer gatherings that tap and
unveil the specifics of His priorities and will.

Hearing God. Revival pivots on the consciousness of His presence which results in hearing from God. It involves a humility and trust that is willing to be personally vulnerable in order stay in the prophetic flow of the Spirit. Operating in the flow of His Spirit and His will, results in the tendency toward remarkable answers to prayer.

Hearing God is always in conformance with the standard of His Truth. Those truly tapping God's guidance are like the Bereans in Acts 17, daily searching the Scripture to verify and grasp all that the Spirit is imparting.

Radical Obedience. Hearing God and obeying is not in any way passive. It realigns and it changes things. It changes things on both an individual and a community-level. It becomes the basis of what is referred to as societal transformation.

It can be said that spiritual maturity kicks in when the prime focus shifts from issues of self to engaging one's calling in serving community and Kingdom issues. Radical obedience accelerates this process. It generates a more global, proactive perspective that is interactive among those sharing in this flow of the Spirit.

Most Distinguishing Characteristic

True revival is marked by the atmosphere of God's presence. It is an atmosphere of His presence that doesn't fade when the gathering is over. It abides. It represents a spark, an igniter of the Spirit which those embracing it carry with them.

What we perceive when "God is moving" is first our heightened God-consciousness, together with a God-response to our spiritual hunger and purity of our reach for Him.

When the atmosphere of God's presence prevails, the dynamic fuels an explosive multiplication. This is the increase that results as the combination of the anointings and the diversity of the gifts of those in the community, responding to revival begin operating together in unity.

Those who have experienced revival, the atmosphere of His presence, yearn for the unfathomable consciousness of His presence. It is insatiable. It has a depth that knows no bounds. It sparks at the dividing asunder between soul and spirit. It is contagious for those who truly seek truth. His presence indeed changes everything.

Revival's Catalysts

There are subtle distinctives that characterize the catalysts that ignite revival, versus the nurturing or maintaining of revival, and then of spiritual maturing.

Sound doctrine helps us mature spiritually as we progressively grasp the glimmers of His Truth. Yet Jesus referred to the Holy Spirit as the Spirit of Truth, Who leads us into all Truth. Holy Spirit revival fires guide us into Truth. Revival is that process of release that provokes the manifestation of the reality of God.

There are some who are carriers of revival. This is a key function of how the anointing operates

Carriers of revival are catalysts, igniters of God's presence. When one spends time in God's presence, they begin to operate as a carrier of His presence. We make reference to "flowing" in His Spirit. The anointing is given release, from the priority given to time spent with God.

When it matures with a pure heart, the overflow of the anointing operates in concert with the leadership anointing, each within their own sphere (2 Cor 10:13). It is the foundation for influence. It has become the basis of many successful ministries. It similarly represents the authority of the intercessor to be a shield for those for whom they stand in the gap.

Moses was a carrier for God's presence. He was a gatekeeper for God's glory among the people. It was a dynamic that began with the time Moses spent in the glory cloud coupled with the fervency he had in reaching to consciously abide in God's presence.

"'I pray You, if I have found favor in Your sight, let me know Your ways that I may know You, so that I may find favor in Your sight. Consider too, that this nation is Your people.' The Lord said, 'My presence shall go with you, and I will give you rest.' Moses then said to Him, 'If Your presence does not go with us, do not lead us up from here. For how can it be known that I have found favor in Your sight, I and Your people? Is it not by Your going with us, so that we, I and Your people, may be distinguished from all the other people of the earth?' Then Moses said, 'I pray You show me your glory.'"
Exodus 33:13-19

Many years ago, during a time of ministry, a man of God prefaced his ministry to us with these words: "I sit in the presence of the Lord. There are many things I could say to you; but what I bring you, I bring from the presence of the Lord." That orientation is one of my chief prayers for what I scribe with my writings and what I impart with my God's economy program.

I have no desire to operate outside that context. I yearn for and seek the anointing that breaks the yoke. In this quest, since the late eighties, I have embraced a lifestyle of arising in the middle of the night to pray and seek God. It is a part of the cost, joyfully paid.

The Kingdom of God is the culture through which God's people operate. Revival and the restoration of God's order are at the heart of the Kingdom. God is a consuming fire. His presence is a catalyst, a fire that ignites change in its wake. When manifesting, this conscious, flowing presence of the Lord, through His people, yields the authority to reset governments and economies and the cultures of the peoples of the world.

At the core of this abiding presence operating through His people, is what Paul referred to as the law of Christ: bearing one another's burdens. Scripture tells us that Jesus took up our infirmities and carried our sorrows. He was bruised for our iniquities and by His stripes we were healed. It is the standard for those willing to endure the cost. It is the banner for those who have been prepared for this season.

It is a mantle of fire traversing a pathway of fire, with a responsibility and authority that wields God's glory to restore His order. It is a mantle that carries a cost for those paving its pathway.

"The wilderness and wasteland shall be glad. The desert shall rejoice and bloom. You shall see the glory of the Lord, the excellency of our God. So strengthen the weak hands, make firm the feeble knees. Say to those who are feeble-hearted: 'Be strong, do not fear.' Then the eyes of the blind shall be opened and the ears of the deaf unstopped. The lame shall leap like a deer and the tongue of the dumb sing. Waters shall burst forth in the wilderness and springs in the desert. The parched ground shall become a pool and a highway shall be there and a road. It shall be called the highway of holiness. The unclean will not pass over it, for it shall be for the redeemed; and whoever walks this road will not go astray." Isaiah 35:1-8

CHAPTER 4

THE DIVIDING LINE

"In the time of the end, many shall be purified and refined, but the wicked shall do wickedly and none of the wicked shall understand; but the wise shall understand." "Those who are wise shall shine like the brightness of the sky, and those who lead many to righteousness, like the stars forever and ever." Daniel 12:3, 10-12

A spiritual shift is redefining the world around us. Many are being purified and refined while wickedness thrives and the blindness of the wicked abounds.

The bar is being raised for God's people. Before us is a time of extraordinary miracles and the discipling of nations. It also will be a time of disruptions and uncertainties, a time of judgment. Straddling the fence will result in being shot at from both sides.

Deuteronomy 30 describes the dividing line: "God has set before us life and death, blessing and cursing." There is a sobering need to make right choices. No more middle-ground. It mandates understanding the times and His agendas with a seriousness of being about God's business. It is a path with a requisite of walking in holiness.

Higher Dimensions

The book of Hebrews admonishes us to leave behind the focus on the elementary things and reach for the higher goals of maturity (Heb 5:13-6:3).

Many are called, but few are chosen. Walking in God's calling is linked to walking in His will. Walking in God's will requires walking in His timing.

Saul was anointed king, but was ruled by the fear of man. He was driven by his passions and he compromised. It was not about him. It was about God's purposes for him being king. He never quite grasped that. Missing God at this level equates with rebellion. At one juncture, Samuel summed up Saul's actions by saying that "rebellion is of the sin of witchcraft." Saul's fears made him prey to forcing issues and being unwilling to wait on God's timing.

The Secret of Abiding

Holiness results from becoming one with the Holy Spirit. It is His righteousness being manifested in our thoughts, words, decisions and actions. It is abiding in Him with a sense of honor that begins by speaking truth in our own hearts, as described in Psalm 15.

Holiness is a life and poise-of-the-soul summed up by the Psalmist when he said, "let the words of my mouth and the meditations of my heart be acceptable in your sight, O Lord." Holiness comes from a heart so tender toward the Lord and His Word that when it recognizes a truth and realizes something is out of alignment, it immediately changes.

Holiness results from a pure heart. It comes from a spirit free from the constraints of the flesh and unholy dependencies. Holiness is a strength and unwavering trust in the Lord in the face of adversity. It is walking through the fire without the smell of smoke.

There came a time in Jesus' earthly ministry when He told His disciples that He no longer considered them servants, but friends (John 15). This time of demarcation was marked by Jesus imparting the truth of "abiding."

Just as Jesus described Himself as being in oneness with the Father, so this truth marked those He had prepared to lead the pathway, as they became uniquely aligned together in Him. This transition took those prepared into the realities of maturity, just as the forerunners of today are emerging into the realities of maturity. Crossing this dividing line releases an amazing dynamic of His fire and power. It is the mantle of fire.

"The works that I do he will do also; and greater works than these he will do, because I go to My Father." John 14:12

Alliances and Coalitions

There is a "strategic" dimension to abiding. It pivots on the Issachar context, but with the twist that the Body as a whole needs to understand the times in order to know what to do. It is holiness that goes beyond the individual dimension and moves in community-harmony in a way that conforms to God's heart and agendas. It is the light set on a hill that cannot be hidden It is the catalyst that will ignite transformation (Matt 5:14).

Joseph and Daniel operated consistently in this level of abiding. The anointing attracts. While they proactively were blessed to be a blessing, they harnessed the community around them in their efforts and fostered alliances with those with whom they served.

It didn't matter whether they were in prison, the lion's den or in the king's palace. Their identity, priorities, goals and responses to circumstances were consistent regardless of their position. They knew Who they belonged to and they were about His business. They understood the authority with which they had been entrusted and they exercised it.

Joseph and Daniel disciplined their hearts to give single-minded focus to the big picture of the Lord's purposes and their part in it. This focus released authority; an authority that changed the spiritual climate around them.

They faced the realities and paid the cost. They were not swayed by threats, pressures or what appeared as the outlook of things in the natural. Their hearts were fixed, abiding and trusting in the Lord, as they fearlessly took the initiative, when they knew the timing was right, to accomplish God's purposes in their spheres.

For these uncertain times, this strategic dimension will mean being connected. Lone rangers and the fear of authority that goes with it will experience unnecessary hardships. Rebellion, as in Saul's misfires will result in sad, untimely forfeitures of what may have been significant callings.

We have moved from the tactical to the strategic. The Body has long been fragmented. Yet, from this point, unity will no longer be something nice to strive toward. It is going to be the foundation for survival.

Alliances and coalitions will emerge, as the God's people respond to the changes unfolding in the world. Strategic alliances will be birthed with modern-day Cyruses and Pharaohs: chosen, anointed non-believers with a heart for God and His people who are gatekeepers into the seats of power and resources in this world.

The New Breed

In concert with this, a new wave of leadership is emerging within the Body. It is a mature, seasoned leadership that operates beyond issues of strife and ego. Daniel spoke of these days and those who would stay the course to be purified and refined. These are the ones through whom exploits will flow. They are the ones to wield the mantle of fire.

They will be facilitators with the gatekeepers. They are a new breed of trusted leaders who extend trust, but with great wisdom. They will be igniters who spark the needed operational balance between the kings and the priests. They will flow in the prophetic and apostolic, as well as in opening the gates for the corporate operation of the ministry gifts.

"The household of God, having been built on the foundation of the apostles and prophets, Jesus Christ Himself being the chief cornerstone, in whom the whole building, being fitted together, grows into a holy temple in the Lord, in whom you also are being built together for a dwelling place of God in the Spirit." Ephesians 2:20-22

The Psalmist wrote: "Lord, You make me wiser than my enemies; I have more understanding than all my teachers, for Your Words are my meditations." (Ps 119: 98) It was said of Daniel and the Israelites who served as advisors to King Nebuchadnezzar that they were ten times wiser than their occult counterparts. These are times in which a new level of wisdom will be seen operating from today's emerging, prepared Josephs and Daniels. Exploits will manifest and abound, exploits driven not by finesse or moxie, but the anointing.

While restoration and holy transformation is being ignited with God's people, the wicked are revolting against God. Not unlike the days of Hitler, the wicked and unsuspecting are attempting to present acceptable spins to their wickedness and covert occult activities.

Despite the darkness and turbulence, those who have been yielded to the preparation will see their light shine and the glory of the Lord will be upon them. From this there will be supernatural increase and "suddenlies."

Numbers 11:25 describes God's means of increase. The leadership of Moses was multiplied – in a day in time – when the Spirit of the Lord that had been solely upon Moses, came upon the 70 elders. For Israel at the time, this was a major paradigm shift.

Moves of God supernaturally multiply the fire of God and His power exponentially. They trigger change and reach into some of the most unlikely sectors of society with God's influence. Holiness and moves of God also are the catalysts for God's judgment.

Judgment and Fulfillment

"Yet now I take courage. For once again, in a little while the Lord will shake the heavens and the earth and the sea and the dry land, and he will

shake the nations, so that the treasurers of all the nations will come in and fill this house with the splendor of the Lord." Haggai 2:4

As the Body faces the dividing line thresholds and embraces holiness, judgment will be released. For the righteous, judgment is not to be feared. Judgment is sent to purify. When it is resisted, it destroys. When yielded to, it becomes a facilitator, an igniter.

Judgment always reasserts God's authority. It will bring fulfillment on levels beyond what the best of human efforts could achieve. From this dynamic the Lord's dominion will be reasserted with a world seduced by its passions, as it revolts against the Lord and His people. So it will be that with judgment will come great authority and supernatural exploits demonstrated by God's people in an awesome outpouring of God's Spirit.

Like in the days of Joseph, God's people will enable opportunity in the midst of economic disruptions. Similarly like told by Daniel, they will shine like the brightness of the sky, as many, as multitudes are led to righteousness. The choices for the thresholds of the dividing line will open spectacular gates for the fulfillment and flow of God's reality and glory.

"The days are near when every vision will be fulfilled. For I the Lord will speak what I will and it will be fulfilled without delay. For the rebellious shall see that I will fulfill whatever I say, declares the Lord. When the people say the visions he sees are for many years from now say, this is what the Lord says, 'none of My words will be delayed any longer, whatever I say will be fulfilled.'" Ezekiel 12:22

CHAPTER 5

THE SECRET THINGS

"In the year that King Uzziah died, I saw the Lord seated on a throne, high and exalted, and the train of his robe filled the temple. Above him were seraphim . . . . and they were calling to one another: 'Holy, holy, holy is the LORD of Hosts; the whole earth is filled with his glory.'" Isaiah 6:1-3

All truth is parallel. Whether in business, in social organizations or within the church, everyone wants to tap the creative, to unlock the secrets that will release opportunity. Steve Jobs was known for this ability. He thought differently and viewed things from a different perspective than most other people. He sought to change the world and within his sphere he did.

Yet, in God, there is more to this dynamic. In God, the bar is higher. It's more than what a focused, ultra high-energy intellect can develop. In God, it involves operating beyond ourselves. In God, it entails a cost. In God, it is ignited by His presence and conforms to the pulse of heaven.

In God, there are complexities to our spiritual environments not only to be aware of, but to be taken on and subdued.

The story of Isaiah's glimpse into the presence of the Lord and the calling that followed unveil secrets in this creative process, a process that goes beyond the normal boundaries of prayer – a process with secrets that will shake the rafters and bring about meaningful change.

Entering God's presence challenges everything around it. Just praying the words of the seraphim angels can put one in touch with His awesome holiness and the reality of the whole earth being filled with his glory.

Beyond Ourselves

Yet to abide in His presence, calls for more. There can be no pretense, no illusions nor the traditions of men. Jesus noted that the gateways of heaven would be open to Nathaniel, as he was a man without pretense. Still, both Deuteronomy and Hebrews describe His presence as a consuming fire. Surmounting these hurdles, God's presence contains a rhythm, a pattern that combines His glory and His nature.

God's presence triggers secrets and mysteries beyond our natural comprehension that give release to His creativity. Touching His presence sets in motion the unlimited dimension of His glory, as His very nature overflows with the creative. The very process sparks change.

As Isaiah was reaching beyond himself and ran into God's presence, God's presence unveiled a secret, which Isaiah embraced. The authority to unfold the creative process followed, as Isaiah's response to his calling released him into becoming a force for change that would reshape everything around him.

The Progressive Rhythm

Isaiah's response made him an integral part of this process, this progressive rhythm, this pulse in God. For those entering this dimension in God, change will result. For the person walking out a calling, the first thing that will happen will be that the perspective will change. It's more than just revelation. It begins inwardly before it can be released outwardly. Encountering God's presence for Isaiah brought the wise reply of: "Woe is me. I am a man of unclean lips among a people of unclean lips." The response of repentance changes your thinking and begins the process.

Solomon had as much to say about fools as he did wisdom. Fools are constrained by limitations in their thinking, by their own revelations. Fools, regardless of their IQs, are those who become obsessed by their own perceptions of reality rather than God's unlimited glory and the process to be unleashed.

A Force for Change

Reaching beyond himself, as Isaiah did, is foundational to maintain the process. Sustaining the process means becoming a force for change. It is the simple things that confound the wise. It is why again and again, God uses ordinary people to do extraordinary things. They are ones who have discovered this rhythm and the gateway into God's treasury of secret things.

The Listening Heart. Maintenance during this process also pivots on listening, a heart intent on hearing His Truth. It's been said that our ability to hear His voice is directly correlated to our willingness to obey it. That explains why meekness and humility are so important to embracing truth. Those who fail to get beyond the inward response, as if it were about them, as well as those who are unable to "hear" due to their own constant clutter of chatter, are going to miss it. Even those who have experienced deep revelation must get beyond themselves and stay there. It takes more.

It is more than just hearing. Jesus revealed a deep truth to this dimension about His presence. He told His disciples that the words He spoke, He did not speak on His own authority, but that the Father did the works (John 14:10). Jesus was constantly pointing back to His dependency on the Father. In unveiling this gargantuan insight, He told His inner circle that He was the true vine and the Father was the vinedresser. From that premise, he imparted the necessity of bearing fruit, needed to keep the process moving forward (John 15:1). Fruit is the natural result of abiding in Him.

The Secret of Abiding. This is the biggest point of stumbling. His presence actuates creative change. It is His nature. Where we fall short of the secret is in being a force for His change. That secret depends on abiding in Him. When we abide in Him, His nature flows within us and the natural course of things will be creative change. It is a place beyond our selves. It involves a faith that will not compromise with evil.

As Isaiah pursued the process, he uncovered a deep dimension in the cost of abiding. He prophesied that the Messiah (Isa 53:4) would "bear our griefs and carry our sorrows." This is a part of the secret in which everything, beginning with the natural order of things, will change. Jesus spent nights in prayer, in the presence of the Father.

During those times, He entered the spiritual world and tapped the realities that would soon follow in the natural. It is where the cost was paid and the transaction sealed. It was in that secret place that He took on the griefs and sorrows and actuated the release from bondages as He flowed in the place of God's unlimited creativity.

"Truly I say to you, whatever you bind on earth shall be bound in heaven and whatever you loose on earth shall be loosed in the heaven."
Matthew 18:18

Operating Domains

Historically, the game-changers among God's people have been those who have learned the secret of abiding and drawing from the pulse of heaven. Game-changers are forerunners, leaders whose influence reshapes the way for others. Progressively, their domains have penetrated the spiritual foundations of society in the world around them. The primary spheres of this game-changing influence include culture, economy and power.

Culture. Long before Joseph was promoted by Pharaoh, to bring sweeping change to all of Egypt, he had a track record of changing the spiritual climate in some very humbling and challenging circumstances. An important part of this dimension was his stewardship and the trust he engendered among those he served. His identity was clearly in God. Challenging the favor and trust as Potiphar's manager, Joseph experienced spiritual backlash in rejecting Potiphar's wife's unrighteous advances. Nevertheless, despite his lack of position in both Potiphar's house and as a prisoner in the jail, Joseph made a significant impact on the culture around him by what he derived from the presence of the Lord.

Isaiah's insight into Messiah being wounded for our transgressions and bruised for our iniquities is the truth that breaks cultural bondages that have held God's chosen captive. The cultural trap comes from transgressions and iniquities. This release is not only from the bondages preventing us from knowing Him, but in being released IN Him. It explains why Isaiah's first burden, the first priority from God's heart, following His encounter with the Lord in Isaiah 6 was in addressing the dullness of the hearing of the people.

Economy. The economic comes from God's nature to bring increase. For Joseph, everyone recognized that it was God that prospered whatever Joseph did. The prophetic wisdom drawn from Pharaoh's dreams not only averted the impact of the coming famine, but was the creative impetus that put Egypt in the drivers-seat when the money failed and the grain they had stored became the only currency with value. In another instance of famine, Isaac encountered God's presence and drew on the wisdom and creativity of God and produced harvests when no else was able to grow anything.

One of the biggest hurdles today for those navigating Kingdom agendas is getting beyond the fund-raising mind-set and tapping God's unlimited creativity and resources. Without degrading the value of community generosity and the need to provide opportunity for others to participate in Kingdom agendas, there are limitations to the fund-raising model, of drawing from the well at the same source.

Among God's people, fundraising has been elevated to almost the status of a sacred cow, of being the catch-all solution. The story of Joseph gives evidence to how, through God, alliances can be created and resources generated that anticipate change and exceed the limitations and expectations of the world around it. It will be a critical component of the wealth transfer dynamic. There is a significant bridge to be crossed in our day designed to open the gates into these unlimited dimensions of God.

Power. The biblical stories of God's people, along with the teachings of Jesus are demonstrations of how righteous power overcomes in corrupt settings. Power is facilitated through leadership. From the beginning, God's people have been endued and anointed as leaders. As a people, the calling has been as a society of leaders.

Leadership, in God, depends on the Isaiah response to Him. It operates by service, influence and by the anointing.

Whether for individuals or as a people of God, the release begins with our mind-sets, our way of thinking. The power and creativity from His unlimited glory begins when we change our thinking and begin renewing our minds.

The real power of God has no boundaries, yet every revival in history has gone through a process in which the unlimited dimensions are squelched over time through institutional and religious thinking. That was the reason for Jesus' sharp encounters with the blind institutional and religious thinking of the religious elite. The power of God is progressive and depends on the ongoing response to His presence and His voice.

Discerning the Spiritual Environment

There are complexities to the spiritual environments around us that far exceed our human abilities to grasp. Yet, in God, we not only become aware of and sensitized to them, but gain the authority to subdue and bring change to these complexities, to the spiritual climate around us.

Joseph did. It began from the bottom up before he was entrusted to work from the top-down. It is why the bar is higher in God. It is why we have to abide and operate beyond ourselves. It is why truth, meekness and righteousness are so essential. It explains the "waiting on God" that so many modern-day Josephs have experienced. It underscores the importance of the prophetic in this process of preparing as a force for change.

Big Picture Prophetic

While all truth is parallel, not all truth is equal. Even within the prophetic, we need to bring the process full circle to where, like Joseph, Moses, David and Jesus, we get the big-picture. Paul said that we see in part. How true for most. Likewise, how true that so many tend to act when the picture is not complete. It bears on the need to abide.

Jesus said very clearly that to find true life, we have to give it up. We have to get beyond ourselves and our limited, staid ways of thinking and begin abiding sufficiently to start tapping the secret things, the strategic, secret things that are needed for this hour. Abiding takes humility.

In Exodus 15 Moses addressed the people, as a whole, with this truth. IF they would just listen and adhere to the voice of the Lord, it would take them beyond themselves to where none of those things plaguing the world around them would make a big difference to them. They would be the game-changers, the force for change. It is the challenge that remains before us.

The whole earth is filled with His glory. When God's glory is at the core of things, creativity will be released by abiding in that secret place. When the abiding amasses, it will be what is needed to be the force for change for which the world is yearning.

"My heart overflows with a good theme, with verses addressed to the King. My tongue is the pen of a ready writer. You are fairer than the sons of men. Grace is poured upon your lips as God has blessed you forever. Gird up your sword O mighty one, in your majesty and splendor. Ride on victoriously, for the cause of truth and meekness and righteousness. Let your right hand teach you awesome things. Your arrows are sharp, the people fall under you. Your arrows are in the heart of the king's enemies."
Psalm 45:1-5

SECTION II

THE CHALLENGE

CHAPTER 6

THE RELIGIOUS SPIRIT

"Blessed is the man who has made the LORD his trust, and has not turned to the proud nor to those who lapse into falsehood." Psalm 40:4

The religious spirit has plagued the thrust of God's people from the beginning. Since the first century church, its counterfeit antics have perverted the household of faith's quest for more of God. Its modus operandi is subtle, seductive and entangling.

At its root is the perversion, the misapplication of the glory and blessing. At its gates even the elect stumble trying to do the right thing for the wrong reason. Its undermining tactics are why, for so many, that the power is either anemic or it backfires.

Combined with mammon, its potential is magnified with an influence bleeding into the infrastructures of culture, economies and seats of power.

The core application of the glory and blessing was labeled by Paul as the law or the principle of Christ (Gal 6:2), which he described as *"bearing one another's burdens."* This core application should be a banner we uphold.

The long-standing foundation of this dynamic is outlined in Isaiah 53:4 and Matthew 8:17: *"Surely He took up our infirmities and carried our sorrows."*

Paul wrote Timothy (2 Tim 3:5) to be cautious in dealing with those who are caught up in themselves with a form of godliness, but whose lives are a denial of God's power. The psalmist (Ps 40:4) describes those who have turned to the proud or lapsed into falsehood. When combined with those who are ever learning without coming to a knowledge of the

Truth (2 Tim 3:7), you have a snapshot of those caught in the grip of the religious spirit.

The Stumbling

The churches in Revelation 2 and 3 demonstrate how communities and institutions of believers can "get it" partially, yet still significantly be blind-sided.

Only two of the seven churches noted garnered the Lord's approval: the persecuted churches in Philadelphia and Smyrna. Part of the church at Thyatira had kept their focus and wasn't seduced and waylaid, like their brethren, by religious falsehoods and devices.

The rest were clearly instructed to repent, corporately.

The pathways into their spiritual slippage included: the presumption of living on past exploits, having lost their original focus and purpose, along with being encumbered with the cares of the world and straying into becoming compromising and lukewarm. At the core of these revealing judgments against the churches missing the mark was a religious spirit, which distorts and misapplies the glory and blessing.

It illustrates the intensity of the battleground within institutions where replacement of the vibrancy and direction of the move of the Spirit has taken root. It punctuates the importance of upholding the mantle and standard that defines true biblical leadership.

It is humbling that the churches judged in Revelation were within the generation of congregational communities birthed by those who had walked with Jesus. Since its inception, one of the most subtle deceptions operating against the church has been in accurately assessing the enemy's actions.

Evaluating the enemy's capabilities by using the same yardstick used to measure ourselves has been the soft-spot in the tactical underbelly for God's people over the centuries. The lure has been in "being like everyone else."

From the beginning God has had His own playbook for His people. In selecting leaders, Moses' father-in-law advised him to choose from those exhibiting not only competence and the fear of God, but those who were truly trustworthy and who had a track record of avoiding covetousness (Ex 18:21). Jesus advanced the secrets from this playbook. They are the principles of the Kingdom.

On an individual basis, there are several key factors by which the religious spirit erodes one's purity of heart. It begins with pride and fear, but simultaneous taps covetousness (greed), deceit, division and confusion.

Paul's prescient response to this fine-line issue is a key Kingdom principle: that in our weakness, God's strength would be manifested. So it was with the two churches gaining the Lord's approval in Revelation. The others in need of correction, in one way or another had aligned themselves to operate on the same basis, using the same standard and criterion, as the world around them.

The Issue Compounded

Christian groups, from churches, to ministries, to marketplace organizations seeking to overcome the world, too often measure their success – and approach their goals as an issue driven by money. In the Kingdom, that is the cart before the horse. In reality it is a matter of stewardship.

The loss of this focus leads to the influence of mammon, whereby the love or quest of money rules. Jesus said: "he who is faithful in what is least is faithful also in much" (Luke 16:10). Good stewardship will prevail in its mastery over whatever resource is truly managed.

However, when the religious spirit is compounded with the love or quest of money, then the gates are opened for disorder, division, critical distrust and an array of controlling, manipulating spirits. Given free reign it digresses into sorcery and the misuse of the anointing by what some refer to as charismatic witchcraft.

Many years ago, the Lord spoke a most unique word to me concerning the business I was operating. He instructed me that: "whatever sphere of influence you walk into, to immediately begin looking beyond it, lest it overwhelm you." While I recognized the wisdom this pointed to in applying the dynamic of faith, this word yielded even greater insight into avoiding the breakdown of stewardship in which either mammon or a religious spirit or both could gain access.

Illustrating this point of stumbling within Christian organizations was a prayer initiative that was birthed when George W. Bush became president. Designed to mobilize and provide the prayer support needed for the national task of wielding righteous power in corrupt settings, it initially blossomed. The realities of supporting this effort required fund-raising. However, as the initiative evolved, the fund-raising began morphing the focus on prayer until the initiative stalled and then fizzled. The means became the end. It was clearly the right thing done in a wrong way.

Curbing the subtle power of mammon begins with the awareness of its devices, even within the context of good stewardship. The ability to make or raise money is not the answer. Parenthetically, those with a true Romans 12 gift of giving hold the most potential in its mastery.

The antidote to this alliance between the religious spirit and mammon begins with pure, singleness of purpose for those over finances wrapped into a foundation of godly maturity, humility/trust and leadership.

The Maturity Factor

In His relationship with His disciples there came a time when Jesus told them that He no longer considered them servants, but friends. Jesus was raising the bar. He said that servants don't understand what their master is doing, but that He had made known to them ALL that the Father had shown Him. With that, He extended trust and imparted the essential dividing line for Kingdom maturity.

It was the point that their calling and their lives were not about them.

"He who loves his life will lose it, but he who hates his life in this world will gain it eternally." John 12:25

Jesus penetrated the spiritual veil (Heb 6:19-20) to embrace the pure power that scatters darkness. This is the process restored. It is the demonstration of the fullness actuated by Jesus' victory over death. This mantle has been passed to those anointed leaders willing to pay the cost and persevere to access the veil and fulfill the law of Christ by destroying the works of the devil. Unfortunately, far too many short-circuit the process and succumb to making an idol out of the calling.

Those genuinely anointed to lead, whether as priests, prophets or modern-day Josephs will wield the glory and blessing needed to walk into the face of darkness with a purity and authority that risks everything, but makes darkness flee.

"Build yourselves up in your most holy faith and pray in the Holy Spirit. Keep yourselves in God's love; . . .be merciful to those who doubt; snatch others from the fire and save them; to others show mercy, mixed with fear–hating even the clothing stained by defiled flesh." Jude 20-23 NIV

The Humility and Trust Factor

The anointing to lead can result in a personal overcompensation for the enormity of the calling. Cindy Jacobs once told me that many true modern-day apostles, which include today's Josephs, operate with a false humility. It is a sign of incomplete preparation. Godly humility cannot be contrived. It is forged in the fire and carries with it a recognizable authority.

Godly humility is devoid of arrogance and deceit as those who recognize true authority serve as pure God-pleasers.

"Lord, I am not worthy for You to come under my roof, but just say the word and my servant will be healed. For I also am a man under authority with solders under me and I say to this one 'go' and he goes and to another 'come' and he comes." Matthew 8:8-9

Stripped of position, Joseph the Patriarch had very little he could depend on, other than the Lord's daily guidance and the authority that came from the mantle of God's blessing that he wielded. Joseph was groomed in a fire of humility to where it became a part of his nature. With the brand-mark of humility was the integrity of heart and trust that he could always be counted on to do what he said he would do.

With his chief advantage being the guidance and wisdom God was giving him, there was little to no room for pride or scheming. That is the foundation required for true spiritual maturity and biblical leadership.

The Leadership Factor

Understanding the significance God had for the role served by Joseph the Patriarch lends a glimmer into understanding the long and very arduous wait-times being endured by many modern-day Josephs.

In raising the bar, Jesus described the criteria for true friendship and love, as the willingness to sacrifice, to give yourself for those counted as friends (John 15:13). He defined friends as those who could be trusted with the details of God's strategies and purposes. That dynamic is the foundation for His standard for love – and with that the real foundation of humility. Without trust, the mantle falls short and is prey to the scheming and selfish ambition provoked by the religious spirit.

Weathering the devices of the enemy's onslaughts against Christian organizations takes both maturity and leadership. Mature, godly, sacrificial leadership will have no other foundation apart from humility and trust. Against such, the enemy cannot stand.

"This is my instruction, that you love one another, as I have loved you. Greater love has no one than this, than a man lay down his life for his friends." John 15:12-13

The Fine Line

God's preparation time for Joseph galvanized him against the religious spirits and sorcery that prevailed in Egypt. That inoculation gave him mastery over mammon in his role as chief administrator of resources in averting tragedy for those under his charge during the famine.

Joseph became the model of a true prophetic steward. His example is the counterpoint to those succumbing to religious spirits who have deviated from the narrow path in their time of preparation.

Entrance into entertaining religious spirits is too often triggered by short-cuts. It takes discipline and resolve to hold the course. Joseph's path into maturity and leadership was enriched by humility and the trustworthiness he exhibited in the years of abiding in God's presence. As it was for Joseph, there are no short-cuts.

This path into abiding with the Lord involves a fine line described in Hebrews as the "dividing asunder between soul and spirit." Perseverance and waiting on the Lord for His established times are not options. They are in fact the crucible that weeds out the many who are called from the few who are chosen.

"The way of the righteous is level and smooth. O Upright One, make the path of the righteous straight." Isaiah 26:7

CHAPTER 7

RESPONSE TO EVIL

"Lord, You have set up a banner for those who fear You, a standard displayed because of the truth. That Your beloved ones may be delivered, save with Your right hand and answer us." Psalm 60:3-5

Mind-sets are a compilation of assumptions that influence how we live our lives. They are the predispositions of our attitudes which determine how we respond to the circumstances around us. Mind-sets shape an individual's behavior. Cultural mind-sets mold the identity shared by a people.

Working with believers in cultures where freedom is at risk has often challenged me to take a closer look at my own individual and cultural mind-sets. One culture I've worked with in particular includes a number of leaders who have spent extended time in hard-labor prisons for their faith. The intent of these incarcerations of brutal conditions was to undermine their faith. It had the opposite effect.

In each case, I've been struck by the strength of character, decision-priorities and genuine humility of these friends who bear these brand-marks of their faith. On the other hand, what I have not observed in the West is the result of the undue focus given to issues that impact the soul. In conditions designed to break their spirit, the imprisonment of these brethren included severe deprivation of essentials such as having enough food to live and the realities of facing death.

Despite such harsh treatment, what I have witnessed has been a distinct absence of a victim's mentality. In lands of persecution, almost everyone has a story of tragedy and serious loss. Yet, contrary to Western predispositions, the choice has been to put their tragic pasts behind them to more fully live in "the now."

"Forgetting those things that are behind and reaching forth for that which is ahead." Philippians 3:13

Paul's admonition is not to "stuff it," but rather to renew our minds and make a choice to transform our thinking by giving focus to remembering those things that are true, noble, just, pure and of good report (Phil 4:8). That is the rallying banner. It is the standard upheld by those we regard as heroes of faith.

Foundations to How We Respond

At the core of the way of the Kingdom is how we respond to evil. Our mind-sets play a significant role in this response. The first premise is that we cannot hope for much by responding in our own strength or cleverness, no matter how much we verbalize it. It takes a great deal more, even for the most talented.

The opening scripture is about that added dimension that only comes through God. It is from a Psalm describing a people who have strayed and lost the power and protection of God against evil. It outlines the need to be restored and highlights what is required to maintain that place in which God intervenes on their behalf.

Over the centuries, the Lord has imparted banners and standards for the good of His people. They serve an initial function to help us avoid the subtleties of evil. When ignored, they still provide the means of deliverance, although at a higher cost when evil inroads can only be met by judgment.

The banner displayed gives first priority to embracing the unequivocal fear of the Lord. That calls for a choice. The standard then sets the stage to unveil the truth and the reality of God that empowers deliverance. It is the foundation from which we can cry out to the Lord and expect the manifestation of His power.

Bondages result when God's supernatural standards are watered down with the natural. Within the Body are many who enjoy God's blessings yet are constrained from crossing the boundaries into what is represented by the fullness of their callings. The constraints typically are self-imposed, driven by precepts of men, with the standards influenced by both individual and cultural mind-sets and predispositions.

The response to evil draws a line in the sand. Not recklessly or arbitrarily, but rather as a choice and a priority to uphold the standard. That choice is contrary to the way the world responds. That sometimes means sacrifice. Yet, that choice is the very foundation that Jesus imparted to His followers during His earthly ministry.

The Subtle Influence

For years I have worked with men and women of God being prepared with modern-day Joseph-type callings. The calling of God in the marketplace is not one of position or status, but a calling of influence. The influence evolves around establishing God's standard against evil, harnessing resources, and bringing deliverance and transformation within the infrastructures of the world's systems.

Yet, again and again the pressures and subtleties faced by these modern-day Josephs bring challenge and distortion to their mantles. With the distractions and deceptions, the result is being drawn into safe-places, of spiritually treading water.

As an illustration of the subtleties that distort and diminish the standard, the Western media has long advanced a cultural mind-set that turns returning military heroes into victims. It has undermined the standard of the cause of freedom with subtle, downgraded and distorted moralizations. The brand-marks of true heroes are then dishonored and reduced to pity.

Pilate's challenge to Jesus was based on this very premise: that Jesus was facing death and Pilate had the authority to release Him. Jesus' response to Pilate was that his authority was limited and defined only by the Father. Figuratively speaking, Jesus spit in the face of death. Jesus was never a victim. His response refused a mind-set of pity, as He held to the standard.

Jesus said He came not to destroy the law and the prophets, but to fulfill, to bring completion to them. He drew a line in the sand with destruction and death. Yet, until the time He was turned over to Pilate and Herod to face crucifixion, the focus of His earthly ministry dealt with the response to evil within the household of faith.

"From the days of John the Baptist, the Kingdom of Heaven suffers violence and the violent take it by force." Matthew 11:12

The Evil Within

The evil within the household of faith is far more subtle than the evil from outside the community of God's people. Ranging from factors such as obsessive introspection leading to majoring in minors and spiritual myopia to outright misuses of authority, the result has long been a people of feeble power, fragmented and divided.

Nevertheless, overcoming these vulnerabilities represents the cohesive foundation needed to maximize the power in responding to evil coming from the world's system. No one group has the total picture, which is why we need one another.

The level to which the evil within the community of God's people is properly addressed will be the level that destabilizes and dilutes the impact of the evil lurking outside the camp.

"Do not be afraid of the sudden fear nor of the onslaught of the wicked when it comes; for the LORD will be your confidence and will keep your foot from being taken." Proverbs 3:25-26

The inroads of evil into the household of faith find their seedbed in mind-sets, the most devilish being religious mind-sets. Instead of being the influencers and overcomers, the Body has systematically become culturally compliant and spiritually anemic. The perception is viewed as the reality. Most purveyors of news are no longer presenting facts, but rather the spin of events within the view of a creeping system of godless values and evil-intended priorities.

In God's eyes, the reality is based on the standard. God's standard is the driver for our mind-sets, the factor that determines what is right and the priorities we ascribe in stewarding our destinies. That standard is then wielded to the degree that our thinking and actions are in oneness with Him.

When God's people are in alignment with Him, His glory will manifest. God's glory manifested when King David brought God's people together. That was King David's greatest accomplishment and will be the standard for the model in the millennium.

To grasp the dynamics needed to realize the release of God's glory in the face of evil requires a closer look at what pride really is, how true humility upholds the standard and the role of suffering. With that is the need to understand how the Word of God defines wickedness within the ranks of the household of faith.

The Seduction of Pride. There is a fine line between pride and honor. True honor comes from God. Pride, however, is self-created and rails against the knowledge of God. Self-righteousness is based on pride. It seduces and distorts. The Bible says that pride is like death and cannot be satisfied (Hab 2:5).

Jesus addressed this dynamic manifesting with the Pharisees. They reached for the standard and missed. Their elitism and self-serving ambition for status and power pushed them away from God. It manifested in the mind-sets and the priorities they gave to the way they lived their lives. Jesus called them hypocrites because of their spiritual myopia.

The history of God's people is filled with stories of "strays" who have misused their authority and operated under short-sighted, prideful illusions of their own significance in their stewardship of God's power. The Bible describes them as wicked.

Proverbs 12:5-7 draws a sharp comparison between the righteous and the wicked. It applies within the boundaries of God's people. The divergence is between being just and operating with treachery and deceit. It speaks of the wicked seeking to entrap, of being ensnared by their own words, while the righteous maintain their integrity despite backlash to emerge not only whole, but with new dimensions of purpose and enlightenment. Remember Job's response to his "friends" and the later end for Job.

"When Job prayed for his friends the Lord restored his fortunes and gave him twice as much as before." Job 42:10

It is the way of the Kingdom to respond to evil with good. In short, the root of the righteous, defined by this standard, cannot be moved or uprooted (Prov 12:3). It emphasizes our complete dependency on God and the importance of humility and a listening heart in maintaining the standard to stay the pathway.

Humility and a Listening Heart. At the core of a righteous heart is the humility that comes from a genuine listening heart. We continually need to be hearing from God and the truth of His Word. We likewise need the wisdom from those who have gone before us as well as the God-fearing whose orientations are not constrained because of their vigilant search for what is truth.

"[The Bereans] were more fair-minded. . . . in that they received the word with all readiness, and searched the Scriptures daily to find out whether these things were so." Acts 17:11

That is not to suggest a potpourri of opinions, but rather a mature discernment of the essentials needed to grasp the biblical standard guiding the steps of the community of faith. The need calls for more than a doctrinal statement on a web-site.

The world we live in, along with today's factionalized Body demands strategic-level wisdom in establishing the scriptural common ground of *how we come together* and *how we operate as the community of faith* – in a way that draws the world.

"You are the light of the world, a city [community] set on a hill that cannot be hidden." Matthew 5:14

The homosexual community mapped out just such a strategy roughly three decades ago. They have exceeded their goals. So it was that Jesus observed that the sons of this world can be more shrewd in operating with their own kind, than the sons of Light. To have a story to tell begins WITHIN the household of faith, with the degree to which we are listening to one another. The common ground involves how we OPERATE together. That will require humility.

Humility toward God and others is a Kingdom key. It is an igniter for unity. Humility is the shield against pride and the fear of man. Paul described the ultimate spiritual enemy we are dealing with as death. True humility inoculates us against the fear of man and the age-old seductions of death and destruction.

The Response and Role of Suffering. People who have faced death in combat and survived, understand the reality involved in face-offs that "cheat" death. Winston Churchill was a man who over the course of his life had many encounters with death. He was intimately acquainted with how evil operated. His demeanor was fearless. His consistently big-picture response was to uphold the standard against evil.

When he was made Prime Minister, what he was dealing with was a faceoff with death. Hitler's machine had conquered most of the European continent. Churchill was surrounded by those seeking to appease evil. As irreverent and as unorthodox as Churchill could be, he was much like a modern-day Cyrus. God knew and called Cyrus long before Cyrus knew there to be such a One as the God of Israel.

In the world of 1940, Hitler may have been the human mechanism, but it was death that was on the march. In its grip were the chosen of God, with the anemic stewardship of the Lord's standard in the crucible. Churchill's response to death, to this amassing evil was to draw a line in the sand. Not unlike King David, with wisdom beyond his own brilliance, he rallied the free world and brought them into unity.

The response involved a time of extreme sacrifice and suffering. Historically, times of great revival have been directly correlated with times of sacrifice and suffering. So it is that we find ourselves today with evil amassing before us.

The Big-Picture Response

These are times described in Isaiah 60 as when darkness is covering the earth and deep darkness the people. Evil has aggressively come out of the closet. The clarion call for the household of faith is to give heed to the big-picture and to gird up the loins of our mind-sets. Humility and listening hearts, along with facing the realities must be given precedence.

The need is to redirect the focus of the energies given to the fund-raising soap boxes, and sweep aside the idols occupying our minds (Ezek 14:5). In responding to the big picture of what is happening around us is the need to draw a line in the sand, calling the evil within for what it is and to begin giving focus to the strategies needed to fully draw on our Great Equalizer in facing the realities.

Peter notes (1 Peter 4:17) that judgment first comes to the household of faith. Jesus said that each would be seasoned with fire and every sacrifice seasoned with salt (Mark 9:49). That is the mix, it is the cost required to be carriers of His presence. In facing the disarray and division, it is time for the household of faith to uphold the big-picture standard, serve as God's calling card, as He draws all men to Himself.

"We have a strong city [community]. Lord, You have established and strengthened our walls and ramparts. So, open the gates, that all who are righteous may enter, the ones who have remained faithful. The steadfast of mind You will keep in perfect peace, because he trusts in You. For in You we have an everlasting Rock." Isaiah 26:1-7

CHAPTER 8

MYOPIC SPIRITUAL VISION

*"When King Jeroboam heard the man of God, he stretched out his hand, saying, 'Seize him!' Then his hand withered and the altar was split apart. Then the king cried, 'Please entreat the Lord's favor and pray for me, that my hand may be restored.' So the man of God prayed for him and his hand was restored. Then the king said, 'Come home with me and I will give you a reward.' But the man of God said to the king, the Lord commanded me not to eat bread, nor drink water, nor return by the same way. So he left by another route from the way he came to Bethel. On the way, an old prophet came to him and said, 'Come home with me and eat bread, for I too am a prophet and an angel spoke to me to bring you back to my house.' So, as they sat at the table, the word of the L*ord *came to the old prophet and he cried out, saying, 'Thus says the L*ord*: Because you have disobeyed the word of the L*ord*, ate bread, and drank water, your corpse shall not come to the tomb of your fathers.'"* 1 Kings 13:4-22

This unique story describes a time of revolt, a time of chaos against the House of David. It takes place, with a shift in generations, in the generation following Solomon.

Solomon's son Rehoboam had ascended to the throne. When he did, across the land the various factions David had brought together sought affirmation after suffering hardship and change during Solomon's reign. Jeroboam had been overseer of the labor force from the house of Joseph. Amidst dissatisfaction verging on an uprising, Jeroboam had fled for his life from Solomon to Egypt.

Change and the Prophetic

On the way, he encountered Ahijah and was given a prophecy that he would be king over the ten tribes of Israel. Yet, upon learning of Solomon's death, Jeroboam wasn't seeking position for himself. Instead he came with an assembly of leaders to appeal to Rehoboam for more equitable conditions. Against the advice of his father's advisors, King Rehoboam took a hard stand against their offer.

With that response, the smoldering division in Israel finally manifested. Then, in keeping with Ahijah's word, a "congregation of the people" made Jeroboam king. This caused Rehoboam to muster an army against the rebellion.

However, when Shemaiah the prophet brought a word from the Lord not to do so, Judah laid down their arms and stood down. Yet, despite the incredible affirmation from two high-ranking prophets and this reprieve; 1 Kings 12:26 reveals a lack of trust and fear in the heart of Jeroboam. He built false altars so that his people would not have to go to Jerusalem to worship. His fears clouded the spiritual vision needed for his mantle of leadership.

The people also heeded to Jeroboam's substitution for the Feast of Tabernacles. Instead of walking into his destiny by upholding or raising the standard, Jeroboam gave into his fears and lowered it. At that juncture, another prophet from Judah came to King Jeroboam and cried out against the altars and prophesied that the altar would be split (1 Kings 13:3). Dramatically, it was.

The Setting's Dynamics

This setting describes a time in which the government of God fell short. Intervening action had taken place by the hand of the Lord through a series of prophets. The story punctuates the critical need for maturity and a big-picture perspective for those assuming the mantles of both the prophetic and that of leading God's people. It also underscores the significance of the prophetic word and the boundaries of responsibility tied to those administering it. It points to the need within leaders for spiritual vision that supersedes "self;" and the perils resulting from spiritual myopia.

Ripples of Spiritual Short-Sightedness

Solomon's digression into spiritual short-sightedness was a prime catalyst for the discontent brewing during his reign. It was the tripping point over which Solomon went from being the man who God anointed with the wisdom to rule and judge His people; to being undermined by the seductive, blinding influence brought into Israel by his hoard of idolatrous wives.

In short, both Kingdom leadership and the prophetic bear an awesome requirement of accuracy within big-picture settings that has no place for half-cocked presumption or short-sightedness.

The young prophet sent to Jeroboam delivered his prophecy with great power, but lacked the wisdom and maturity to impart the big-picture restoration God intended in this encounter; and he paid with his life.

Serious Times

We've entered serious times. One of the major challenges for spiritual leaders today is talented people operating on their own abilities, with a bit of wisdom and anointing thrown in. It's the cart before the horse. Without proper spiritual maintenance and ongoing, mature spiritual vision; the momentum of past exploits will grind to a halt.

In today's spiritual environment, it requires more. On matters concerning the Kingdom: it's not what you can do for God; it's what you allow Him to do through you. (2 Cor 12:9; Heb 11:34)

Recent prophetic words describe a diabolical unleashing of blinding confusion that internally infiltrates and manifests as division. This division undermines the authority tied to administering the PURE prophetic word needed for societal transformation.

This high-level demonic activity targets the fertile turf fueled by arrogance and spiritual self-satisfaction among Christian leaders. Its subtle snare is releasing a mix of the destructive intent of the "accuser" (Rev 12:10) and judgment into the household of faith.

The initial impact of these stratagems is a spiritual myopia such as was evidenced in the lives of Solomon, Rehoboam, Jeroboam and the young prophet in the opening scripture. When allowed to mushroom, as it was then and is today, the result is ugly with manifestations of organizational and community-level division.

More of the same harder will not work. Along with maturity and a big-picture outlook, the cloak of humility represents the most strategic counter-response for those with mantles of the prophetic and leadership of God's people bearing on societal transformation. Moses, whose impact with the prophetic and transformation extends to this day, was known as the most humble man on the earth (Num 12:3).

"He must increase, but I must decrease." John 3:30

Variations of Spiritual Myopia

When spiritual maturity for the task falls short, spiritual short-sightedness can gain entrance in seemingly innocent ways.

Broad Catchall Applications of "the Kingdom." The Kingdom is not a synonym for church or ministry activities. It is God's authority to employ righteous power in corrupt settings. It is the power of God that releases societal transformation. Its principles, as taught by Jesus, are paradoxes to the way the world employs power.

What Has Begun in the Spirit Being Worked Out in the Flesh. A subtle seduction comes when results deemed "successful" evoke self-satisfaction. The distinction is a fine line between operating in the Spirit and yielding to the flesh.

Add-ons to the Prophetic. It takes maturity and seasoning to recognize the boundaries between a word received and simple embellishments due to the attempt to give "clarity." It is why in most cases the one receiving a prophetic word should not attempt its interpretation.

Jumping to Conclusions with the Prophetic. The other side of the add-on temptation is getting a pure word, but then jumping to conclusions or trying to fit it into a limited understanding or mind-set with a teaching or explanation that may undermine its original potency or intention.

Limitations of Cultural/Doctrinal Mind-Sets. Within the Word of God are the principles needed for life and godliness. Then the Bible has countless real-life examples that demonstrate the models, mandates and wisdom needed for the application of these principles. These principles and models give us a universal wisdom that transcends generations and non-Biblical cultures and mind-sets.

A Void in the Prophetic. Historically, one of the hardest requirements for God's people has been in waiting on Him. Sometimes the most spiritual thing that can be done in a storm is to take a nap. Jesus did (Matt 8:24). Prophetic words, as in the case of Joseph's dreams, often need to mature and await set times. Impulsiveness, embellishing a genuine word and an array of other digressions that short-circuit a maturing word are the causes of more misfires than is prudent to recount.

The Temptations: Provision, Power and Purpose

Navigating accurately with the spiritual begins by recognizing the primary temptations that divert it from its full impact.

Preceding the time Jesus imparted the keys of the Kingdom to a select group of followers, He encountered three temptations. Surmounting each of these areas is essential corporately, for the prophetic and for leaders, in order to avoid short-sighted tendencies in the employment of righteous power in corrupt settings.

These dimensions address the foundation needed to bring change: provision, power and purpose.

When the evil one challenged Jesus with *"command that these stones be made bread,"* the issue involved authority over provision. When the challenge was *"throw yourself down for He has given His angels charge over you,"* it was the foundation of power. Finally, when shown all the glory of the Kingdoms of this world and being offered *"all these things I will give to you,"* the matter addressed the purpose.

These are the dynamics operating with big-picture, corporate-level spiritual matters. They were in evidence in the evolving process leading to Joseph's and Daniel's roles in harnessing Egypt and Babylon for God's purposes.

Provision, power and purpose are at the heart of the issues of societal transformation. Each represent pivot points for apostolic, community and prophetic leaders needed to gain full authority when operating as society-changers; as the ones bearing the mantles of modern-day Josephs and Daniels.

The Maturity Factor

Provision, power and purpose are also key factors bearing on community-level maturity. They are the dimensions with the leverage for change, for good or for bad. They can be the seedbeds for short-sightedness or the foundations for the spiritual vision needed for transformation.

In the opening scripture, it wasn't because the young prophet was beguiled by the old prophet that he was gobbled by a lion. His myopia was an obsession with his return; of confusing the sign of his failure, as being his path to safety. In other words, he was gripped with fear; and what he feared came upon him.

Although Scripture doesn't elaborate, the context and this short-sighted misfire are strong indications that he didn't get the original word quite right in the first place. At the point when the King was open to his correction, his spiritual myopia blinded him. It bore on the "purpose" factor for which his maturity for the task was lacking, AND he was judged within the framework of his myopia.

Reaching for Spiritual Clarity

The attack against the Body today targets maturity bearing on the prophetic and leadership for transformation. Again, the subtlety of the challenge facing the Body is talented people going on their own abilities with an element of the anointing spliced in. The demarcation into maturity will pivot on humility and be Spirit-driven.

Spiritual maturity is not our limited perception of being right or doing right. It is when those matters, we refer to as ego, issues and self, have no root from which to manifest and true spiritual vision can manifest. It is the discernment that knows the difference in the close calls between His will and what may be blind-spots or matters kindled by the soul.

Spiritual maturity on a community-level basis is when there is an alignment of the provision, power and purpose among those deemed as leaders.

Spiritual maturity and spiritual vision enable God's Light to shine and disperse the blindness, confusion and short-sightedness. It releases the Kingdom power that paradoxically transcends the division and reverses it into opportunity. It is when there is no vestige of variation between His will and our own. Spiritual maturity with spiritual vision is a complete oneness with the Lord.

"Unless a grain of wheat falls into the ground and dies, it remains alone; but if it dies, it produces much grain. He who loves his life will lose it, and he who hates his life in this world will keep it for eternal life." John 12:24-25

"I did not come to bring peace but a sword. For I have come to set a man against his father, a daughter against her mother and a man's enemies will be those of his own household. He who loves father or mother more than Me is not worthy of Me; and he who loves son or daughter more than Me is not worthy of Me; and he who does not take his cross and follow after Me is not worthy of Me. He who finds his life will lose it, and he who loses his life for My sake will find it." Matthew 10:34-39

CHAPTER 9

SAFE PLACES

"My people have become lost sheep; their shepherds have led them astray. They have made them turn aside on the mountains; they have gone along from mountain to hill and have forgotten their resting place." Jeremiah 50:6

T he world we live in has changed dramatically. Turbulence has been amassing with an increase of the hazardous. The impact of media-spin just adds fuel to the fires of the realities.

Getting the Focus Right

Yet, in the midst of all the global economic and power shifts and hurdles, Israel faces realities tied to its very existence. It begs the question of the matters receiving our attention amid the gathering sea changes rife with information pollution.

The issue involves rightly discerning our tactical thrust so to be poised and prepared for the Lord's instructions for next steps in this time of change.

The opening scripture from Jeremiah deals with just such a topic: getting the focus right. It places a high standard on spiritual leaders cutting through the distractions in establishing right priorities for the sheep for whom they are responsible.

The spiritual leaders have the duty to prepare and equip their people tactically. They also are responsible for the wisdom needed for the places of rest. These are the safe places needed to be refreshed and properly poised to anticipate and respond proactively and strategically to God's "next steps," the consequent shifts, along with the continual onslaught of evil schemes.

"He will deliver you from the snare of the fowler and from the deadly pestilence. He will cover you with His feathers and under His wings you shall take refuge; His truth shall be your shield and buckler. You will not be afraid of the terror by night, nor of the arrow that flies by day, nor of the pestilence that stalks in darkness, nor of the destruction that lays waste at noonday. A thousand may fall at your side, and ten thousand at your right hand; but it shall not come near you. Only with your eyes shall you see the recompense of the wicked." Psalm 91:3-8

The Age-Old Context

The context for Jeremiah's prophesy was God's judgment on Babylon and Chaldea. Babylon and Chaldea represent the age-old alliance between mammon and sorcery. This unholy alliance goes back to the days of the Amorites, when fallen angels produced a defiled race whose DNA railed against God and His people.

All this was compounded by the subsequent infiltration-advice given by Balaam to Balak. This dynamic has been one of the evil one's repeated strategies over the centuries. Its intent has been to weaken God's empowerment of His people and redirect the anointing to work against them.

This is what manifested with the infiltration of the Nicolaitans in the early church, whose doctrines and deeds began polluting the truth and power of the Kingdom message so central to the early church.

"'And I will repay Babylon and Chaldea for all the evil they have done in your midst,' says the Lord." Jeremiah 51:24

"The evil done in your midst" points to this subtle infiltration. It targets the tares among the wheat. Jesus notes a time when His angels will be sent to remove the lawless offenders. God's judgment is His strategic-response on the Babylon-Chaldean alliance. The impact is designed to amplify the tactical efforts of His faithful warriors.

"With you I will shatter nations and with you I will destroy kingdoms." Jeremiah 51:20

Today's Response to the Realities

So as this day approaches, what is the pathway and the response of those called by His Name to facing today's global realities?

Jeremiah's prophesy was couched with some hard words for the priorities being given by the leaders. They not only missed the mark, but they made God's people vulnerable to the enemy's schemes. They failed to provide the focus and with that, the safe places, places of rest needed to be ready for God's subsequent steps. These are safe places employed during times of great turbulence. These are the safe places from which God's people will advance.

At the core of Jesus' message were the principles on how to employ Kingdom power in a corrupt world. These were not intended as defensive measures, but rather the proactive means to overcome the enemy's schemes and to advance the Kingdom.

These principles do not conform to the way the world exercises power. They require something more.

Jesus clearly stated that He had come to destroy the foundations of the devil's works. It involved the demonstration of the Spirit and power. Like Jeremiah, Jesus spoke words of judgment on the focus and blindness that described the shepherds of His day. With His victory over death, the balance of power shifted. Those he had trained were empowered to turn the world upside down. They did.

The Stewardship of Power

The enemy's behind the scenes battle then was redirected to target the stewardship of power. Power can be seductive and the mantle of shepherding God's people carries high responsibility. Shepherds have a mantle designed to prepare and equip God's people, not as followers, but as a band of leaders prepared for the changes of the times.

The task of leading the sheep beyond being followers is significant to God's purposes. The Gospel accounts outline a sequence of Christian maturity. Beginning with being a follower, one progresses to disciple, then servant. Servants graduate to be friends of God, with the design for them finally becoming the sons that all creation awaits.

Idealism has never lacked in being the seedbed for prime candidates for the defiled counterfeits, even within the context of the Body. Maturity brings the right focus and the discernment to expose the infiltrators.

Over the centuries, every people and nation has responded in one way or another to the bondage that has long gripped the world. Wielders of power have generated a range of mass movements, national, social and religious. Counterfeit movements have produced the zealotry of the Judases, the Nazis, the suicide bombers and those innumerable sheep following a range of causes for change to doomsday prophets.

The enduring solution will only come through God. The realities of this hour give sobering evidence of the need to advance in maturity beyond the confines of followers and disciples. The issue for the Body is getting the right focus and priorities for the saints to steward His power.

Mobilizing and preparing the saints to deploy is central to this stewardship of power. Such deployments require the seasoning and anointing that combine maturity and consecration. The undefiled maturity and consecration needed for Joseph's alliance with Pharaoh was significantly more than that required in his stewardship in Potiphar's house. So it was with Jeremiah's prophecy about the aimless, loss sheep. So it will be with God's judgment against the Babylonian-Chaldean alliance and the polluted infiltrators embedded amongst God's household.

The Gateway

The task hinges on the shepherds breaking the mold of the illusions of success in ministry, properly assuming the calling to lead by serving and then embracing the Kingdom mantle to lead the sheep into the unpolluted realms of truth, the places needed to spiritually and maturely discern the realities and strategies clearly.

The gateway to these unpolluted regions of truth is His presence. This is the place of unfettered peace in which we abide in Him. In indicating that He was the door of the sheep, Jesus unveiled that He was the good Shepherd, that safe place where we learn to abide. He told us that He would not leave us as orphans, but would send the Holy Spirit to abide with us,

"Because I live, you will live also. At that day you will know that I am in My Father, and you in Me, and I in you. He who has My instructions and keeps them [abides], it is he who loves Me. And he who loves Me will be loved by My Father, and I will love him and manifest Myself to him." John 14:19-21

In this same sequence in John, Jesus told us that with the Helper, the Holy Spirit would come His peace.

"Peace I leave with you, My peace I give to you; not as the world gives do I give to you." John 14:27

Fully grasping the significance and extent of His peace is critical to abiding in His place of rest. When Israel played the harlot with the Moabite women and bowed down to their gods, a man called Phinehas interceded and made atonement for the Israelites.

This act touched the heart of God. The Lord spoke to Moses to tell Phinehas that because of Phinehas' zeal for God's honor among his people in making atonement for them, that the Lord was making a covenant of peace with Him. It was a covenant of a priesthood that would extend to him and his descendents throughout the generations (Numbers 25:10-13).

Isaiah 53:5 refers to this peace with the Messianic prophecy of: "The punishment that brought us peace was upon Him." Malachi also referred to the covenant of peace.

"My covenant was with him, one of life and peace, that he might fear Me. So he feared Me and was reverent before My name. The law of truth was in his mouth, and injustice was not found on his lips. He walked with Me in peace and equity, and turned many away from iniquity." Malachi 2:5-6

His peace is in His presence. It triggers oneness with His heart, the mercy that intercedes when judgment is at hand. His rest is what brings sanctification.

"Surely My Sabbaths you shall keep, for it is a sign between Me and you throughout your generations that you may know that I am Yehovah-Mekiddish, who sanctifies you." Exodus 31:13

The setting described in Jeremiah's prophecy is the setting reflected in many segments of the Body across the globe today and even more so in Israel.

The setting among God's people is replete with "zeal without knowledge" as described by Paul. Far too many are on very low batteries spiritually-speaking. Some are burned out due to lack of maintenance for the level of zeal with which they are operating. Some are burning out because they are running with twenty and thirty-year old operating instructions and they need a fresh word from on high for today's times. Far too many are in a condition that is blind to the enemy's schemes to distract and deceive.

Distractions and deceptions breed discord, division and vulnerabilities in facing the realities. On the other hand, the maturity that fosters truth and His peace provides the firm ground for the pathway to provide the seasoned and empowered responses needed for the challenges and tribulations Jesus foretold for this hour.

The Model

The setting for Acts 15 was a time of great turbulence and change. The leadership reflected by the Apostle James is a model for the days upon us. When Barnabas and Paul shared with the gathering about the miracles they were experiencing among the Gentiles, the leadership was being confronted with something that challenged their doctrines and traditions.

The messages given to the churches in Revelation add to these insights. They point to the snares: from the persecution imposed by imposters hating true believers to the embedded infiltrators within: the Balaams, the Nicolatains, the Jezebels. In times of change the bar of the mantle for leadership is raised.

Leading God's people into safe places has nothing to do with avoiding tribulation and turbulence.

From the father's heart evident in James in Acts 15 we realize that it has everything to do with hearing His voice and being prophetically in tune with the flow of the Spirit. It has everything to do with pruning tradition to make way for the restoration of the ancient truths that will demonstrate His power. It has everything to do with searching the Scripture to grasp the implications that the words of the prophets have on the change underway. It has everything to do with the sanctification and consecration needed to close the gates to the infiltrators in order to mature, prepare and deploy the saints for the work of the Kingdom.

"To Shebna, I will throw you away violently and there you will die. On that day, I will call my servant Eliakim. I will clothe him with your robe and strengthen him with your belt. I will give your responsibility into his hands. He shall become a father to the inhabitants of Jerusalem and the house of Judah. The keys of the house of David I will lay on his shoulders and what he shall open no one shall shut and what he shall shut no one shall open." Isaiah 22:17-22

CHAPTER 10

THE ANCIENT CHALLENGE

"Go through, go through the gates, clear the way for the people; build up, build up the highway, remove the stones, lift up a standard over the peoples." Isaiah 62:10

The response to God's presence, of knowing Him, releases a challenge. That challenge is a mandate for change.

The response to the ancient challenge has been the spark to the drama of the ages. It has been the igniter by which good has progressively overcome evil. It is the challenge entrusted to those discerning the keys and entering the gates that employ the righteous authority of the Ancient of Days.

"Bless the Lord, O you His angels, who excel in strength, doing His word. Bless the Lord O you His host, you ministers of His who do His pleasure. Bless the Lord all you His works, in all places of His dominion." Psalm 103:20-22

The Central Issues

At the crux of this age-old drama have been game-changers, leaders with alliances both from within and outside the community of God's people, whose righteous response to His standard would advance His purposes.

"Who says of Cyrus: he is my shepherd and he shall carry out my purposes." Isaiah 44:28

This advance has been demonstrated with strategies impacting the infrastructures of culture, economies and power. Yet, the most important elements for historians: God and His chosen people Zion have largely been ignored in recording the story of man. Understanding the times and knowing what to do rest on a realistic grasp of the historic strategies employed by God and His chosen.

Abraham established the community model for God's people to live in self-sufficiency, as a people of God. Isaac gleaned the secret of God's economy and supernaturally prospered through God, despite the impact of famine. Joseph demonstrated how stewardship that abides in God's presence can influence the spiritual climate of a society and release God's authority within its infrastructures, to overcome impending evil and to accomplish God's purposes.

Moses provided the framework for the Abrahamic model to inoculate itself from the subtle wickedness of the surrounding world and become a society of the righteous, living for God. David demonstrated the leadership response to God's guidance needed to shape a society of diverse factions into a Kingdom of God's people, that would prompt awe for God and His people from all those around them.

Jesus raised the bar to the ancient challenge and opened the gates to the authority that governs cultures, economies and seats of power. In so doing He set the Kingdom standard for applying righteous power in a corrupt world.

The Core Dynamics

Isaiah declared (Isa 43:10) that God's servant, His people Israel, were chosen as witnesses to know and to demonstrate what it meant that He alone was God. Through that mantle, God's standard progressively has been raised.

Paul wrote the Romans (3:2) that the chief advantage held by the Jews has been and is in being entrusted with the oracles of God, which include His standard, His ways, His intentions and His utterances.

The birth of Christianity was not a new religion, but rather the fulfillment of the ancient pathways and mandates that began with Abraham. God told Abraham to leave his family and country and the spiritual environment of his ancestors and go to a place in which God would begin a process of fulfillment and restoration. Abraham heard and believed God, and he obeyed.

Through Abraham and His seed, the ancient powers of the Creator have progressively manifested to lay the foundations, releasing God's original intentions.

It is the ancient challenge and mandate for those willing to align their identity and destinies with Him. The oracles of God have opened the way to the ancient powers through which the Lord has and will manifest and employ His chosen to resetting the spiritual climate with change impacting all within their domain.

The Game-Changers

Each generation has had its game-changers, ranging from those anointed and appointed by God, to the counterfeits whose agendas serve evil's intentions to undermine the purposes of God. Each impact the equilibrium and mix of culture, economy and power.

Abraham Lincoln's role in freeing the slaves in America countered the prevailing winds of incredible opposition with what was right and righteous. What played out in the years following the resulting conflict, for which he died, dramatically impacted the culture, the economy and seats of power. It sowed seeds of righteousness that would trigger God's agendas, involving God's people, in the decades to come.

The rise of the modern-day Zionist movement is an example. It is significant in understanding this age-old conflict that the birth of the Zionist movement took place in the same generation as the emergence of the communist movement. The contrast between the fruits of Theodore Herzl and Karl Marx reflect the intensity of this battle of the ages.

Influence of Spiritual Movements

Juxtaposed against the flashpoints of conflicts over the cause of righteous freedom has been the catalytic role served by specific movements of prayer and revival. These are movements that have released change that has reset the foundations tied to God's long-term purposes.

They underscore the significance of the role of God and His chosen in grasping the true central issues of history. It's why the enemy's minions have fought so viciously to have these insights expunged from the annals of history.

The time preceding the US Civil War was marked by an outpouring of the consciousness of God's presence that impacted businesses and communities across this new nation. The influence of the Second Great Awakening gave rise to the manifestation of numerous religious and humanitarian movements which transcended the decades prior to the freeing of the slaves. It countered unrighteous and blind standards marking the status quo, and the lawlessness and chaos that came with America's early growth. The abolitionist movement was one of its results.

Yet, for movements to impact the dynamics of culture, economies and power requires an anointed game-changer who will not bend with the onslaught of unpopular opinion or personal ambition.

The Matrix for Change

Just as important as getting history right, with God and His chosen at the core, so it is essential to understand the cycle and complexity of the matrix operating.

It begins and ends with the spiritual. The igniter for change, as it has been over the ages, is when the prayers of the righteous, aligned with the heart of God, push back against evil. God's presence begins manifesting in response to fervent prayer, with the initial impact spreading across the community of God's people. As the spiritual climate begins shifting, the foundation for advancing change is released.

When the overwhelming consciousness of God's presence takes root, it builds to the level of revival, a manifest move of God. Revival not only changes all within its path, but it plants an influence of spiritual ripples which trigger transformation and gives birth to supernatural dimensions within society itself over the time that follows.

"Then the house, the house of the LORD, was filled with a cloud, so that the priests could not stand to minister because of the cloud, for the glory of the LORD filled the house of God." 2 Chronicles 5:13-14 NASU

It is significant to understanding the power of this dynamic, that those ministering to the people in this passage were unable to stand due the awesome consciousness of God's presence.

The Second Great Awakening, the abolitionist movement, the US Civil War, the reshaping of societal and business foundations during reconstruction and then the Zionist movement significantly restructured cultural, economic and power structures. This snapshot of the matrix of change is only one example.

The mix of isolationism and appeasement in the 1930s gave rise to evil atrocities against freedom in general and God's chosen specifically. Ultimately the spiritual forces clashed with WWII. A great rise in the focus of prayer from a broad sector of society was progressively released.

The momentum of concerted prayer not only brought a righteous conclusion to the conflict, but in 1948 Israel, against all odds, became a nation. Remarkably in the same year came a healing revival that released a still greater outpouring of prayer and hunger for God's presence.

As the dynamics of this matrix amassed, 1967 became another such time in which the purposes of God and the presence of God converged into movements and events affecting God's chosen. It was a time of concentrated spiritual climaxes. Included in these events was an unusual flashpoint of war in which Israel for the first time in centuries, regained control of Jerusalem.

It was in this same year that the charismatic renewal was birthed, a time in which the consciousness of God's presence was making a great impact on the non-believing. This was also the year giving rise to the Messianic Jewish movement, a time from when more Jews have met their Messiah, than in all the years since the Lord walked the face of the earth.

During this same timeframe, Christians began mobilizing and strategically advancing their efforts through the use of the media. The extent of the ripples of change in the decades following has been dramatic, as have the struggles for freedom, as new layers of evil have been uncovered and pealed back. It has all stemmed from the buildup of gathered prayer, God's manifesting presence and a stand against evil.

The Keys Releasing the Ancient Challenge

The igniters of concerted prayer and the matrix of change release the ancient challenge. From the earliest church fathers came the prophetic mandate to rebuild the tabernacle of David (Acts 15:16). The prophecy referred to by James in Amos 9:11 as the tabernacle of David describes God's presence residing among His people. It is the dynamic with its foundation in amassed prayer that released the outpouring of the Spirit described in Acts 4 and opened the gates to the Gentiles. It is the catalyst for change.

When the matrix begins culminating, the momentum of prayer releases movements that bring change that confronts evil and reshapes society around it. At the forefront are leaders like Abraham, Joseph, Moses, David and Jesus, who become one with God and His purposes.

Jesus explained this destiny-shaping dynamic to His followers.

"At that day you will know that I am in My Father, and you in Me, and I in you. He who has these instructions of Mine and keeps them, it is he who loves Me. And he who loves Me will be loved by My Father, and I will love him and manifest Myself to him." John 14:19-21

The early church began a time of restoration of God's presence being manifested among His people. The conflict became fierce, but from that time everything changed.

"Great fear came upon all the church and upon all who heard these things." Acts 5:11

Historically, the traditional response to gathering evil too frequently has been either collaboration or appeasement. God's standard does not mix with either. The ancient challenge takes a stand and goes against the grain despite the onslaught of opposition.

The world has reached just such a flashpoint.

Over the centuries, the key factor shared by those answering the ancient challenge as game-changers has been their ability to abide in God through the firestorms. Proverbs reveals that the man who rules his own spirit is mightier than the one who can take a city. To the point, Jesus said if we would have faith as a grain of mustard seed, God's purposes would take root.

A frequent question concerning the calling of modern-day Josephs has been "when will the time of the Josephs manifest?" The answer is the same as it was in the days of Joseph the Patriarch: "When God speaks to Pharaoh." However, the prelude to God speaking to Pharaoh will be shaped by the amassing of prayers and steadfast faith demonstrated by the stewardship of the Josephs.

There's a shaking taking place all around us. God is allowing the box to be rattled so that we begin looking outside-the-box instead of at ourselves. The time of Joseph was a time in which God's plan was much bigger than the status quo and the inbred, self-righteous, as well as short-sighted religious, ambitious thinking of God's covenant people. The role of game-changers will not be limited to the parameters of the "box."

With evil coming out of the closet today at unprecedented levels, the challenge, as it has reemerged across the centuries, is for God's people to take a stand and give heed to mobilizing prayer that brings forth His presence. With that will be the emergence of the leaders whose influence impacts cultures, economies and power to embrace this mandate of the ancient challenge.

The time of the Josephs is at hand. It will be a time in which the identification and alliances with modern-day Pharaohs and Cyruses and other strategic gatekeepers will be significant. The time of the Josephs will be a time in which the gates of the world's systems will be penetrated for the Lord's purposes.

Abraham Lincoln's leadership example provides wisdom for today's genuine Josephs. His attitude was consistent: his mission was not about him or his popularly or fame. He was a game-changer willing to fully face the onslaught of opposition. Today's Josephs are those prepared, who will embrace the ancient challenge and steward the mantle of fire to wield the mandate for change.

"Life up your heads, O gates and be lifted up O ancient doors that the King of Glory may come in. Who is the King of glory? The Lord of hosts He is the king of glory." Psalm 24: 9-10

SECTION III

THE PATH

CHAPTER 11

SEASON CHANGES

"That which has been is what will be, for there is nothing new under the sun." Ecclessiates 1:9

Despite Solomon's prescient grasp of the cycles of the times, he lost his focus. His priorities became muddled. Under his reign, the seeds were sown that undermined Israel's season of unity, peace and prosperity that had been engineered by his father.

From the beginning, the age-old struggle of evil's intent against good rears its head at unexpected and subtle junctures. The foundations shift as the times change with new generations. While God has provided the wisdom to build from one generation to another, new generations cannot simply ride the momentum. Again and again over the centuries, during times of spiritual slippage, evil has enveloped God's people, seeking to destroy them.

On the other hand, the Lord has always had His Davids, His champions, who would risk everything to stand against evil and prevail.

"I have found David the son of Jesse, a man after My own heart, who will do all My will." Acts 13:22 NKJV

During this last generation, there has been an incredible dismantling of the assaults of evil against God's people; ranging from the fall of Nazism, to a standoff of the onslaughts against God's people in Eastern Europe, Russia and Asia.

Many champions have stood and resisted, some at the cost of their lives. *"A Song in Siberia,"* by Anita and Peter Deyneka (1977, out-of-print)

is a gripping account of the severe persecution against believers in Russia during the 1960s. Many excellent accounts have described the plight of the church in China during the Cultural Revolution. The spiritual struggle of God's people, as cultures within cultures, has again and again reemerged in this recurring struggle between good and evil.

In this last generation, God's chosen champions have wielded His mantle and strategy and undertaken the risks and the burdens on behalf of the brethren walking through the fires of persecution. They have heeded the heart of God in walking into the heart of darkness to destabilize and thwart the intents of evil. They have wielded God-strategies to pierce the darkness resulting in many miraculous spiritual climate shifts.

The Simple Things

In God's way of doing things, it has always been the simple things that confound the "wise." In the early 1970s, a gospel singing group and band known as the Living Sound accepted an invitation to conduct a concert in Poland. What they and their founders, Terry Law and Larry Dalton, didn't realize was that the invitation had come from the Communist Youth Party and that their performance was to be at the organization's headquarters.

When they arrived, their hosts realized the group's spiritual foundations. Serious flashpoints followed, which included its leaders being interrogated and threats given to try to prevent their "witness." Still, with an overflow crowd already seated, the concert took place. The anointing and God's presence pierced the atmosphere. Hearts were deeply touched. Members of the audience lingered long beyond the concert, until after 3 a.m., as the team prayed for and led great numbers to the Lord.

What followed from that concert was a chance meeting with a Catholic Cardinal (Karol Yozef Wojtyła) who subsequently opened the doors to Living Sound for another concert in Eastern Europe, this one with over 100,000 in attendance. This Cardinal went on to become Pope John Paul II.

Restoration in the Face of Darkness

These events were strategic. They were a part of the change of seasons underway at that time. They were a part of God's strategy to break the stranglehold of the brutal persecution against His people. The spiritual climate change that resulted became a part of the spiritual restoration and strategies that has since changed nations.

Subsequently, within another season change, as the iron curtain was falling, a similar and parallel strategy emerged. This strategy targeted the "lost sheep of the House of Israel." Jonathan Bernis, along with the Messianic Jewish praise group, Kol Simcha (Joyful Noise), began identifying key strongholds in Eastern Europe, the Former Soviet Union and other lands, in which to hold stadium-sized festivals to attract the persecuted Jews of these areas. Our first God's economy workshop was for a vibrant Messianic Jewish congregation that was birthed following one of these festivals in Eastern Europe.

What began with our first God's economy workshop has been a part of God's strategies. These efforts taken to targeted groups of the persecuted and oppressed have exceeded chance expectations in the way they have taken root. That's because they have been a part of these initiatives, birthed by God, to restore His people in lands of persecution.

Diverse but Parallel Streams

A wide range of brethren from diverse segments of the Body responded to God's heart during those days with effective and parallel strategies to assist the persecuted.

I spent many years on the board of a ministry, in which one of its founders, during the days of the Iron and Bamboo Curtains, made many dangerous, yet timely, undercover trips into "closed-access" nations to impart words of wisdom, to pray with, and to encourage the leaders among the persecuted brethren.

In instance after instance, I recall that within months reports of changes came, that exceeded human capabilities. They only could have been the result of the Hand of God. These divinely ordained connections with those who many had forgottten, like the efforts of Living Sound and Kol Simcha, were matters very close to God's heart and as such, an important part of His strategies to change the balance of power for His people. It is notable that initiatives were birthed during as well as following, days of revival.

The Shift

Change results when communities of God's people, as a whole, fervently seek Him. When that fervency wanes, darkness finds subtle inroads. Historically, the seedbed for revival is either a time of deep moral darkness, national depression or severe persecution. While evil's seeds of destruction provoke these factors, when amassed and combined with God's people truly seeking Him, they trigger God's judgment.

"While following the way of your judgments, we have eagerly waited for You. At night my soul longs for You. Indeed my spirit seeks you diligently.

For when the earth experiences Your judgments, the inhabitants of the world learn righteousness." Isaiah 26:8-9

Now, at the change of a generation, which has so incredibly rolled back the tentacles of persecution in lands defying religious freedom, has come a creeping evil. Its target is the foundations of religious freedom in these free societies.

The right response of God's people in times of both persecution and creeping evil is a fervent focus on God's ancient standards of seeking Him. When that takes place with broad consistency, God releases strategies for change. God's strategies spark miracles. God's strategies penetrate darkness with tangible spiritual climate change.

However, with the waning, has come a shift in the spiritual tempo of our times. With that shift in the spiritual tempo, has come a shift in strategies. A subtle message for "free societies" is coming from brethren in lands of persecution, who have paid high costs for their religious freedoms. The message taps the shift in strategy for lands of "freedom," where evil subtly, but systematically has been eroding religious freedoms.

Responding to the Shift

Responding strategically to the tempo of the times requires a war-time mind-set. It demands the courage of Elijah to confront evil and a willingness to risk all. It calls for repentant, forgiving hearts with an acceptance of the diversity represented in the various streams comprising the Body. These factors carry the need for a maturity that reflects the discipline to diligently seek God and His priorities, with a revelation of our identity in God, that we are who God says we are. As such, we penetrate the darkness as a light shining on a hill that cannot be hidden.

A War-Time Mind-Set. Far too many within the Western Church have become complacent to the systematic erosion of both righteous standards and the freedoms at the foundation of our society. It is time to draw a line in the sand. There is a war underway that is both spiritual and cultural. There is a critical need to embrace a way of thinking, a war-time mind-set that responds in a manner parallel to the days of WWII, when our very freedom was in jeopardy.

Elijah-Level of Courage to Confront Evil. Elijah put his life on the line in confronting the prophets of Baal and Asherah. Yet, it wasn't done arbitrarily. It was God's strategy and Elijah was God's champion to draw the

90

line in the sand. Elijah not only brought judgment upon the perpetrators of the spiritual erosion evident among God's people, but he demonstrated the reality of God to bring restoration to those who were being subjected to the seductions.

Sacrificial Hearts Poised to Quickly Repent and Forgive. During war-time, the expectation is for everyone to be sacrificially operating with and moving toward the same objectives. That requires hearts to be right before God together with those with whom we live and work. We cannot afford the luxury of being offended. We need one another. One of the primary indicators of this type of heart is the readiness to repent when wrong, along with a heart that quickly forgives.

Maturity to Grasp the Essentials of Common Ground. Maturity and being of one accord go hand-in-hand. We work on doing that with those we consider kindred spirits, those with whom we choose to worship. However, there are many streams within the Body with many significant, yet diverse functions. None have the full picture. Yet, we need to understand the essentials, the primary things, representing the common ground of our faith and to embrace a respectful acceptance of the functional and even doctrinal diversity that is comprised within the Body.

Discipline to Diligently Seek God and His Heart Priorities. War-time requires great discipline and sacrifice on the part of all. That begins giving our first priority to our time spent with the Lord. Seeking God should always be our first priority, but the reality is that there is a tendency toward slippage that comes during the comforts of peace-time settings. The discipline required to diligently seek God's heart and align ourselves with it is critical for this change in seasons.

Unequivocal Identity in God. It takes an unequivocal revelation of one's identity in God to survive the brutalities of persecution. That means understanding what God's Word says about who we are and what our role is in this world. That viewpoint should define our priorities. The root of our standing strong in the fire of adversity begins with our identity in Him. That requires a proactive renewing of our minds with His Truth and an interactive prayer life that has a foundation in Psalm 15, of speaking truth within our own hearts.

The story unveiled in "A Song in Siberia" gives evidence of how congregation after congregation, at great personal cost, embraced the essentials of Kingdom priorities with one accord. Leaders were jailed. Some were martyred. Despite that, new leaders came to the plate. Against all odds, they prevailed. The fire of persecution not only melded them together, but became a demonstration, a witness, of the reality of God that shouted at their neighbors. Great numbers came to the Lord because of the faithful response of the believers, to God and to each other, despite the harshness of the persecution.

Strategies for New Seasons

Jesus gave a strong admonition to be alert to the signs of the times and the change in seasons (Luke 12:54-56). The US is divided. Russia is advancing its territories. Rogue states are thumbing their noses at the West. Terrorism and lawlessness abound without boundaries. Alliances of totalitarians and Muslims threaten the stability of the free world. In the face of these developments, those emerging from years of severe religious persecution are a model for us, in lands where freedom and culture are now at-risk.

Jesus came to refocus things, to restore the true foundations for those whose identities are in God. He came to raise the bar. So it is today, that the bar needs to be raised. Jesus came to give us the tactical means to pierce the veil and establish God's domain, His Kingdom, resides in what the Apostle Paul referred to as "the bondage of corruption" and what Pope John Paul II famously referred to as "the culture of death." So it is today, that there is nothing new under the sun.

Centuries ago, God spoke to Abraham and told him to leave his family and his nation. What he left was the land of the Chaldeans, the heart of sorcery and the occult. Today, we face a similar time of demarcation, a change of seasons. We need to call the culture of death for what it is: the occult seedbed for activities of Satan. We need to recognize that our lives have been bought with a price and that our citizenship is first, as God's people.

The core message from those emerging from the fire is one of stewardship. The call in facing the fire is to prepare and make the decisions of life, as if our freedom might be lost, but to pray fervently to preserve those freedoms, and to live our lives with a first-priority faithfulness to God and to the brethren, so that those around us will recognize the difference.

"The servant who knew his master's will, and did not prepare himself or do according to his will, shall be beaten with many stripes." Luke 12:47

CHAPTER 12

THE UNSEEN

"Do you hear the secret counsel of God, and limit wisdom to yourself?"
The book of Job 15:8

Throughout the Word of God, reference is given to a dimension described as "secret." The secret place is most frequently used to refer to God's presence. The secret things allude to God's wisdom. Job points to the secret counsel of God.

These dimensions are likewise described as the hidden and the unseen.

Jesus taught that prayer works effectively when we get alone and pray to our Father, who is in the secret place. The NIV version of this passage depicts the Father as the One who is "unseen."

"But when you pray, go into your room, close the door and pray to your Father, who is unseen. Then your Father, who sees what is done in secret, will reward you." Matthew 6:6-7 NIV

Paul illuminated this nugget of truth in his letter to the Corinthians with his admonishment to give focus, not to the seen, but to the unseen.

"So we fix our eyes not on what is seen, but on what is unseen. For what is seen is temporary, but what is unseen is eternal." 2 Corinthians 4:18 NIV

This dimension being referred to is the spiritual.

Despite being beyond the normal human perception of things, the "unseen" is foundational. It drives the reality we live in rather than the other way around. Our grasp of this dimension provides insight into the priorities we select in our pathway of life.

Applying the Unseen to the Seen

The unseen dimension is the distinguishing characteristic of those we characterize as the heroes of faith: ordinary people doing extraordinary things by means of applying the unseen to the seen, through God.

During his time in Egypt, Joseph bridged the seen with the unseen. In spite of his position as a slave in Potiphar's house, he made a significant difference. The scripture in Genesis 39 indicates that everyone recognized the difference operating through Joseph. They saw that the reality of God accompanied Joseph and made all that he did to prosper. Joseph effectively wielded the mantle of his great-grandfather Abraham: to be blessed to be a blessing. The means toward this end has always been in bridging the seen with the unseen.

I like being around people who bridge the gap between the seen and the unseen. Yet, I have experienced backlash, just as Joseph innocently experienced spiritual repercussions with Potiphar's wife, as something beyond the seen challenges us operating in the unseen.

This process and what is unleashed challenges the focus which resides solely in the seen. It can trigger the forces of darkness, which seek to usurp and bypass the dimension of the unseen controlled by God. It can be deadly.

Within the unseen are the realms of the real and the counterfeit. Reaching for the unseen that is truly God extends beyond the natural and human realms. It involves a process. It is a process of unfolding dynamics which challenge both the counterfeit and the seen. The process begins with individuals, but evolves to be facilitated by the community. When this process is traversed according to God's standard, it releases God's glory. The process defiled or short-circuited triggers the counterfeit.

Operating in this domain bears uniquely on the choice of being a God-pleaser rather one whose destiny conforms to the ways of man or to the trappings of power that sidestep the Lord.

The Dynamic Operating

2 Kings 6 describes the king of Syria being troubled, when it was recognized that on each occasion that he sent out his army against Israel, that they walked into an ambush. He surmised that there might be a spy in his inner circle. However, his advisors explained it was the prophet Elisha,

who was discerning their secret plans and then warning the king of Israel. Through God, Elisha penetrated the unseen realm.

This is one of the reasons intercessors need to prevail in unraveling the burdens they carry, to get past the seen, in order to gain a grasp of the unseen, in order to know what to do. Many years ago, I was in prayer. I kept having bad thoughts concerning a certain person. I initially thought I might have had a hidden attitude toward them and began praying in an effort to correct it. Then the Lord spoke to me and told me what I was sensing was that they were speaking against me.

I was skeptical about this premise and asked the Lord for a scripture to confirm that this was so. In the same hour, I began my regular Bible reading and came across the passage in Ecclesiastes 10:20 that admonishes: "Curse not the king or the powerful in your bed-chamber, not even in your thoughts, for winged creatures will make the matter known."

The unseen realm is where both the angelic and the demonic operate. Those with backgrounds or encounters with the occult and witchcraft understand this reality. It explains why Jesus taught His followers to seek first God's Kingdom, along with His standard of righteousness. God's Kingdom has its foundations in the domain of the unseen.

"Bless the LORD, you His angels, who excel in strength, who do His word, heeding the voice of His word. Bless the LORD, all you His hosts, you ministers of His, who do His pleasure. Bless the LORD, all His works, in all places of His dominion." Psalm 103:20-22

There's a reason that Paul, operating within his apostolic mantle, refers (1 Cor 13) to the two primary dimensions of tongues, as tongues of men and of angels.

The Entrance and Cost
Entrance into the unseen arena comes only at a cost. That cost requires a choice, an ongoing choice and a discipline to stay the course. Joseph's high calling carried a requirement beyond his already significant prophetic gifting. It necessitated a wisdom and authority beyond anything he had previously known.

It called for the harnessing of the resources of Egypt to avert the impact of the judgment triggered by his brothers. Joseph's brothers self-righteously, but deceitfully and dishonorably, broke covenant and sought revenge against Shechem for defiling their sister Dinah. Dishonor defiles what honor establishes in covenant.

95

The issue of honor is essential in navigating God's dimension of the unseen.

"Jabez was more honorable than his brothers. So Jabez called upon the God of Israel." 1 Chronicles 4:9

The story of Job is a story of honor. Job, as God's emissary, begins with Job having only a superficial grasp of the honor needed as God's representative. Zeal is not enough. Personal accomplishment while acknowledging God is not enough.

Like Joseph, Job had to be stripped of his superficial exploits to be able to truly wield the mantle he bore. In that process, his spiritual eyes were opened to the unseen that he had never before grasped. It is a dimension requiring a total dependency on God.

The manner in which Joseph was so abruptly thrust into Egypt gave him every reason to give up. He had every reason in the natural, or the seen realm, to turn his back on God and the unseen, which had caused him to lose everything, including his freedom. Yet, Joseph chose to press into God more fully.

While yet a slave in Potiphar's house, Genesis 39 tells us, that everyone saw that the Lord was with Joseph and made ALL that he did to prosper. Joseph walked out the principle of "bringing every thought captive" to God's standard and will. Despite his circumstance, he put into practice the mantle of his great-grandfather Abraham in being blessed to be a blessing. Without position, he did so honorably and righteously.

These consistent choices of honor and the discipline they require are the mark of true Kingdom leaders.

Harnessing the Imagination

Taking every thought captive involves harnessing the imagination. Jesus gave extremely strong warnings about not allowing your anger or lusts to run rampant in your imagination. James alludes to the dangers of jealousies and selfish ambitions. The imagination holds great potency and is the bridge into the unseen dimension.

This taps the truth that James gave to be doers of the Word and not hearers only, who deceive themselves. Living in the seen alone is not enough. It's more than personal exploits. Walking out a call of God requires the gap to be bridged into the unseen and then walked out in the seen.

Going onto the Offensive

Years ago, I served in a Marine combat unit that went deeply into enemy territory. Tactically, we were trained and disciplined to move about largely unseen. These real-life experiences imparted a wisdom that the Lord has revealed to me to apply in intercession, in spiritually navigating through enemy territory while remaining hidden.

When the unseen is fully embraced, the result will be a moving onto the offensive. It doesn't happen immediately, but takes time and faith. Yet, it will override the seen and the counterfeit. Jesus said, if you have faith as a grain of mustard seed, nothing will be impossible to you (Matt 17:20).

The unseen also requires appropriate authority. By the time Joseph faced the baker and wine-taster when in prison, he possessed the know-how and authority that operated deeply in the hidden realm. Going into enemy territory, discerning and preempting the enemy's intentions, and setting the stage for God's counter-purposes sometimes call for obedience that only "sees" the next step. Yet, this dynamic is strategic to this hour, in preparing the way for those who follow.

Prevailing in the unseen world means discerning, from God, the path to be taken from what is revealed. God always imparts strategy to those willing to pay the cost and prevail in this dimension of reality.

"The angel of the Lord encamps around those who fear Him and delivers them." Psalm 34:7

God's purpose is for the community of his people to be restored to operating in this dimension. This will be the result from what Jesus referred to as being a light to the world, a community set of a hill.

The Community Dimension

Moses wasn't just speaking to an elite inner-circle when he gave the instruction to listen carefully to the voice of the Lord and do what is right in His eyes. He was speaking to the entire community.

When the community begins bridging the seen with the unseen, God's glory is released. When that dynamic prevails, the first evidence will be the spiritual climate changing.

As this dimension of reality gains momentum, then God's converging purposes and priorities will align. The consciousness of God will become evident to even non-believers. What we call revival then begins manifesting.

When revival manifests, the unseen has penetrated the seen. As this spiritual dynamic gains increase, it ignites a high-level flow of unity driven by a broad obedience and flow of the Spirit. This release of God's glory, orchestrated by the Spirit, overcomes evil with good, with the common ground of His glory manifesting and the supernatural becoming natural

When the Life of God within a community truly manifests, it goes beyond a warm feeling or a pristine doctrinal focus. It is Life itself and cannot be stopped.

The Bible is full of stories of prophets, priests, kings, apostles and everyday people who penetrated the unseen and refused to turn loose, and by prevailing they changed the course of history for God's people, setting the stage for eternity.

Abraham staked all on bringing the unseen into the seen. Joseph restored the promises to God's heritage and blessed Egypt in the process. Moses made the connection and infused the truths of his insights into all future generations of God's people. David did all the Lord expected of him and connected the seen and the unseen and in so doing, brought God's people into kingdom unity. Jesus bridged the gap, giving His life as an example to those who would grasp this dimension, establishing the foundation to restore God's original reality for all eternity.

"The secret things belong to the Lord, but those that are revealed belong to us and to our children forever." Deuteronomy 29:29

CHAPTER 13

TOUCHING THE DEPTHS

"Oh, the depth of the riches: both of the wisdom and knowledge of God!
How unsearchable are His judgments and unfathomable His ways!"
Romans 11:33

During His earthly ministry, Jesus made a very profound statement to His followers. He told them that He had come to send fire on the earth and how he wished it were already kindled; but that He had a baptism to be baptized with and how distressed he was until it was accomplished (Luke 12:49).

Jesus' earthly ministry progressively laid the foundation and model for the fire He mentioned and the baptism this fire requires. It is the model for those embracing the call of being His followers.

From Deuteronomy to Hebrews, God's presence is described as a consuming fire. Jesus' presence progressively unveiled this dimension of the anointing, of being a carrier of God's presence. God's power is an outworking of the consciousness of His presence.

Simultaneously, John 1:5 reveals that darkness was unable to comprehend His presence.

There is a cost to stewarding God's presence. It is the cost for displacing darkness. It taps the depths that transcend the natural and for that matter, darkness. Jesus paid that cost at the highest level and changed the spiritual code governing the earth.

The cost begins by completely yielding our lives for His. Jesus said: "He who loves his life will lose it; but he hates his life in this world will gain it for eternal life." (John 12:25) Jesus understood the sacrifice that lay before Him. It was the price and the pathway into which Jesus admonished His followers to "follow Him."

His death and resurrection fulfilled all the covenant promises and God's intentions for His own. It opened the gates to the potential for all His followers to become aligned with and one with God's heart.

Entering the Depths

From this "baptism of fire" that Jesus went through, He gave His followers, those willing to pay the cost, the keys and strategies to enter the depths, this dimension of reality. They are the keys to employing righteous power in corrupt settings. From these depths comes the change that shakes nations.

In 1997 we met a most unusual woman of God named Agnes Numer. Born in 1915, Agnes was older and spiritually more seasoned. She had an equally unusual ministry that had at its core, the feeding of the poor. Her ministry was a faith ministry, simple in its execution, but profound in its impact.

Her efforts had no formal fund-raising program. Yet it consistently fed and housed its active contingent of workers and visitors. It was birthed after she had hit the age of 60; after what she described as years and years spent in her "prayer closet;" following a time she had memorized almost the entire book of Isaiah.

The Dynamics

At the time we met her, her ministry Somerhaven, had several simple things that distinguished it. First, it was devoted to *God's heart for the needy (Isaiah 58)*, in daily sending out two 18 wheelers filled with food for the poor across her state.

Agnes' facility was also *a safe-place* where leaders came to get perspective from God and be refreshed. It was a safe place because *the presence of the Lord* was there. While there were regular meetings for prayer and for worship; it was clear that Agnes was the catalyst for God's prevailing presence at that place.

Agnes' wisdom and anointed prayers were sought by leaders from across the globe. She would receive phone calls in the middle of the night from around the world, from leaders seeking the flow of the Spirit in which she walked. She remained active until the time of her graduation from this earth when she was 95. Agnes was a carrier of God's presence. She was a carrier and catalyst of revival.

We have entered a time, when those, prepared like Agnes, are being mobilized as *carriers of God's presence and of revival*. Their presence will create the spiritual sparks that nudge others out of their status quo.

True revival is a foundational threat to the status quo. It challenges and displaces darkness. Characterized by the power of His presence, its depths are beyond the boundaries of human dimensions and descriptions.

The Equalizer

In more places outside the West than not, people fear the powers of darkness. They fear and give homage to the powers of corruption. Even within circles of believers, the unspoken response can be that the devil is the prevailing power, with God's minions operating as comparative weaklings.

Yet, in our work around the globe, we have been uniquely blessed in working together with ones whose identities and callings are uncompromised against the forces of Babylon and Chaldea (Jer 51:20). They have touched the depths. We've likewise touched and been touched by an infrastructure of ones who hold significantly potent keys to what the Lord is doing in their nations and then globally.

These are ones whose common ground impels them as doers of the essentials of God's heart, along with flowing in the outworking of His presence. Untouched by the approval of man, personal ambition or the trappings of power, they produce spiritual ripples with roots that go deep.

The balance, between the agendas of God's heart and flowing in His presence can only come from the Spirit. One without the other will digress into deception and fall short. Simultaneously, together they are unstoppable.

The crux demands a grasp of applying this unique dimension of the anointing, together with the discipline of operating within the confines of God's set-times in applying His strategies. Stated alternately, in terms I have previously expressed: "It's not what we can do for God, but rather what we allow Him to do through us."

God's Strategies and Opportunity

For communities of believers bridging the gap with the broader community, one of the most effective strategies to maintain this balance and to release this anointing involves food.

Throughout the Bible are spiritually significant instances of eating together or of the provision of being fed. The practice has involved times of settling differences, making peace and establishing agreements.

Similarly, are the instances in which God's people are the catalysts of provision when the world encounters famine and judgment (Isaac, Joseph). In the same fashion, the biblical mandates of the feast-days have their foundations in God's people coming together and eating, as they are spiritually refreshed and strengthened.

These are God's strategies that give opportunity for His presence.

Jesus' time with His disciples repeatedly describes significant spiritual times involving food and eating. From multiplying the loaves and fishes, to the disciples on the road to Emmaus, who after being with Him, only recognized Jesus in the breaking of bread, to Jesus feeding the disciples on the shore after His resurrection; again and again His power and presence find release through the provision of and the breaking of bread.

Within Agnes' ministry, along with feeding the poor, there was always ample food for those assembled and with that food, a fellowship that centered on the Lord.

Years ago, Carol and I began and led a home gathering that met on Saturday evenings. It was designed as a setting for the unreached international community of our city. It began with an hour of worship and prayer. We then would break for an array of international dishes brought by those attending, who also brought their unchurched friends.

People enjoying plates of food would stand around in small groups, discussing lives, needs and the Lord, many praying for one another, often leading members of their group in prayers ranging from repentance to needy requests. Because of the unique answers to prayer that the unchurched attending received, those gathering swelled to over 50. One month we had 16 people from this group who, having seen the reality of the Lord, got baptized in our church.

Gatherings with meals have served as strategies to effectively penetrate spiritually hardened cultures. I know of many instances of believers in tough spiritual climates having actuated change in the hearts of guests through the hosting of meals that included the simplicity of praying for their guests.

In each case, God's presence was revealed. From the beginning, in God's order of things, it has been the simple things that confound the wise.

The Challenge

Having ministered in over 20 nations constrained and ruled by the forces of darkness, the issue involves tilling the spiritual soil that cover the roots of darkness and simply releasing His presence. Sometimes the barriers can be broken with nothing more than the simple request: "May I pray a blessing over you?" or "How can I pray for you?" to "May I speak a (prophetic) word of encouragement to you?"

While in Afghanistan in May of 2002, visiting with a high level government minister of that nation, a bond of trust was created with our small group, when Barbara Wentroble opened the doors, with permission, with a "word of encouragement" to this man. He recognized and embraced it for what it was, a good word from the Lord. While the gifts employed may be different, they each serve to challenge the spiritual status quo with the goodness of God enabling His presence.

It is in the simple things that the depths are revealed. There is an intimacy and bond that comes from sharing a meal.

During our younger days, when our older kids were in high school, I established a practice on each Saturday of taking one of them out for breakfast. It was an opportunity, one-on-one, to listen and to close the gap on matters that made a difference. One summer, my nephew stayed for the summer, so I included him in this practice.

The first time we met, I sat there staring at him as he gave undistracted focus to digging into the array of tasty items on his plate. I finally stopped him with the words, "Look, this is not about food!" Well, actually it was, but I needed to pull back the superficial in order to allow the entry into the depths. From that, came some really meaningful chats. Years later, as an adult, he shared with me the impact that those words and those times and what was released following them, had had on his life.

Touching the depths begins with opportunity that allows the consciousness of His presence. When that takes place, everything else realigns to the extent to which we then become carriers of His presence.

The Power from the Depths

What we refer to as miracles, in reality, are manifestations of the impact of the consciousness of His presence: the parting the Red Sea, Elijah calling down the fire, Jesus casting out demons, healing the sick and raising the dead. With His presence, darkness flees.

The consciousness of God's presence is both the end and the beginning in knowing Him. It is also the reality imparted in making Him known. At the same time, with His presence is His power, albeit the application of His power being the most contested, not to mention misunderstand dimension of God since the days of the early church.

Whether as individuals or as a people, the constraints of man's spiritually-fallen condition limit our natural perceptions of the realities tied to an unlimited God. What we refer to as revival is, in short, a piercing of those constraints, as His conscious presence manifests to those, who together, have touched and held-on to this dimension of the reality of God

"To the eyes of Israel the appearance of the glory of the LORD was like a consuming fire on the mountain top. So Moses entered the midst of the cloud, as he went up to the mountain." Exodus 24:17-18

CHAPTER 14

UNLOCKED

"I will place on his shoulder the key to the house of David; what he opens no one can shut, and what he shuts no one can open." Isaiah 22:22 NIV

Just prior in this sequence of scripture, the prophet had spoken words of judgment against a leader who had fallen short, who was misusing the authority of his office. In establishing his replacement, a unique mantle was bestowed, with an authority that dovetailed with that of David's line, an authority to lock and unlock spiritual gates.

David's greatest exploit was in overcoming the divisions within the community of God's people and aligning them to pursue God's Kingdom purposes, as one. That factor is the substance of a genuine Kingdom leadership mantle.

The significance of rightly shepherding God's people is illustrated by this Isaiah 22 story of the mantle being stripped from Shebna and then bestowed to Eliakim. The change involved one whose stewardship, on behalf of God's people, fell short as it passed a subtle threshold, losing its focus – from its design to mobilize and align God's people – to Shebna becoming obsessed with power and the personal benefit from his position.

A full grasp of the scope of this Kingdom leadership dynamic is vital to the preparation of the Body needed for this hour. It is vital to wielding the key to unlocking the bondage of corruption and releasing the transformation that affects societal change. It is key to employing the mantle of fire.

The Hurdle to Unlock

One of the biggest, if not the biggest gap in the Church today – is the need for something practical and engaging, to enable each believer to WALK OUT A CALL OF GOD.

We've emerged at a change of generations with a "me-too" orientation. We've confused the tactical with the strategic. We've made models out of what may have been simply successful stepping stones for a time, stepping stones never intended as the standard or the model to be followed. Short-sighted misuse of tactical means for strategic ends can impede the unlocking and passage into new gateways.

Volunteerism, for example, is not an end in itself, but rather the steps in the path toward its adherents correctly identifying and then being prepared for release to walk out their own callings. Mimicking success, instead of following the move of the Spirit, of the cloud by day and the fire by night, can be a trap. It impedes maturity within the Body needed to rightly discern and engage in God's strategies for the times.

The blind-spot at the core of such subtle snares is akin to the downfall of Shebna, of becoming in-bred and self-serving. This deception short-circuits the big-picture purposes of the Spirit. The momentum for this misaligned zeal is driven by the overuse or misapplication of early-stage successes and priorities.

This in-bred myopia can breed lone-ranger congregations. Progressively misaligned priorities result in a failure to interact with, pray with and work together with other believers within the surrounding community. It waters down the important factor of how we seek the Lord together. It results in falling short in mobilizing God's people to discern and walk out the calling of God for the day at hand.

In-bred myopia masks the keys needed to unlock the strategies needed to avoid the mix between the collisions taking place due to the "me-too" and "Shebna empire," lone-ranger, short-sighted expenditures of energy and anointing.

There have been almost overwhelming inroads of darkness operating within our cultures, seats of power and economies. However, as God's people, we have a disproportionate advantage. David identified and unleashed that advantage.

The goal is the alignment and mobilization of a people who become the true demonstration of the reality of God for which the world longs. The strategy was soundly implemented by David. Its dimensions are so significant that reference is given to them from the Prophets, to the Book of Acts, to Revelations.

These dimensions are referred to as the key of David and the taber-nacle of David.

The Mantle of David

David's role in overcoming all the strife and division – in bringing the community of God's people together carries significance very close to the Father's heart. It is the standard for the Kingdom. It is the standard to release Body maturity. It represents the crux of turning, the key that unlocks the power in which Light disperses darkness.

This unlocking is also uniquely tied to another dimension tied to the mantle of David, referred to as the tabernacle of David. The tabernacle is the place where God's presence resides. Yet, this dynamic embraces much more than the warm glow from worship. Worship is certainly a significant part, but again is a means to an end.

The goal is the progressive consciousness of God's presence that guides the community as a whole, and becomes the pathway through which the community is built and serves as a Light on a hill.

It is when the infectious reality of God's presence results in the unified community itself becoming spiritually contagious, that the attention of the surrounding community is attracted, being drawn into its sphere. When in operation, it overwhelmingly challenges the gatekeepers of darkness.

The Impact of Unity and God's Presence

Acts 15:12-17 tells of a time of major turning in the early Church fol-lowing Jesus' resurrection and the outpouring of the Spirit, when a move of God began the unlocking of gates, which previously had been locked. A very key part of this unlocking was opening the gates for the Gentiles to partake in the promises long held by the Jewish people.

"So open the gates, so that those who are righteous may enter." Isaiah 26:2

It was a time marked by the reality of the wonders of God's presence. This was another gate unlocked in which the anointing became available to all who believed. It was a time of true revival, a time in which believers and non-believers alike, recognized and were being drawn by God's mani-fested presence.

A great fear of the Lord fell upon not only all the church, but also upon all who witnessed and heard about these things (Acts 5:11; Acts 6:8; Acts 8:6). It was a time when the impact was described by members of the world, as "the world being turned upside down" (Acts 17:6).

Scripture (Matt 24:36; Acts 1:7) refers to set-times determined by the Father alone. Paralleling the above examples from the early Church, we have entered times strategically mapped out in the heart of God. Since the time of the resurrection and outpouring of the Spirit, God's people – both Israel and the Church – have encountered new things, sovereignly unlocked by moves of the Spirit.

Israel's 1948 Independence and then regaining control of Jerusalem in 1967 are modern-day examples. Each was tied to new gates of revival and unity in God's move toward the reestablishment of His order in the cultural, power and economic systems. Today, Israel and the Church are poised before another such unlocking.

The Model for Preparation

So, what are the steps to preparing for God's next steps of progressively unlocking the cultural, power and economic systems? Avoiding the Shebna blind-spots and embracing the keys given Eliakim begins with the preparation needed for ALL to be fully engaged in walking out their callings. It begins in being prepared as a culture within a culture in being led by the Spirit to impart Life in the infrastructures of the world's systems.

The preparation has got to dispel the unscriptural premise of the sacred and the secular that categorizes and separates ministers from the laity. The sin of Shebna, was also the sin of the Pharisees. Jesus' choice of those He drew together as His closest followers broke the mold for religious leadership with his cross-section from every walk of life. These everyday people included people of business, professionals, military leaders, government employees, people of past-disrepute and people of society.

It challenged the premise of a distanced, leadership-elite and raised the bar for service and responsibility, along with extending the mantle of leadership to the community as a whole. With the big-picture model of God-centered, economic community development employed from the days of Abraham, leadership is the influence from everyday people operating in everyday domains for the common good. The key to unlocking these next gates will begin with the preparation needed to break the mold to release entire communities.

The Preparation

In the early 1970s, I left what was in its own right a calling, in order to prepare myself in the pursuit of a higher calling. Having spent almost eight years as a US Marine, I hungered for the opportunity, for the rest of my days, to be used by God.

There were steps in that process. As new Christians we were blessed to attend a church led by a man of God who opened to us the riches of God's Word. Then as we became immersed in the application of God's Truth, together with wise counsel, we were released and sent forth to prepare for entrance into God's plan, as I became a student at Oral Roberts University.

While the academics provided a discipline and depth in learning how to rightly divide the Word of Truth, there was another, very essential and practical dimension. At the core of ORU's mandate is training up young people to hear God's voice to go where God's light is dim.

So the academics were only one part. Together with mentorships and a process of coming to know God and His heart, we were given the foundations for walking out a call of God. Functioning in a vibrant, interactive community, we were given the basics needed to live and maintain a lifestyle of faith, of being led by the Spirit.

The Nurturing and Application

Within this setting was a strong foundation in the living Word. The greatest influence on my future calling was the interactive nurturing that came through God's Word, the testimonies, the times of praying with and the wisdom imparted by ones with their own track record in successfully walking out a call of God.

This foundation and nurturing became the launch-pad for the real-life applications in discerning God's guidance and then stepping out in faith – to walk out the calling and pathway that lay before us.

The simplicity for this preparation was demonstrated by Jesus' nurturing and application of the teaching He imparted to His inner circle during His earthly ministry. The process was very practical. There was teaching, observation and then real-life applications.

Jesus spent nights in prayer seeking the Father as His followers observed His life and how he ministered to the people. Jesus taught His disciples the basics of applying faith, prayer and how to apply righteous power in corrupt settings. The key in this process is the word "application." Jesus taught His followers to be doers of the Word and not just hearers.

Then there came a time when He released them. It was a significant transition. Jesus told them that no longer did He consider them servants, but friends. Friends are those you trust. Friends are ones with whom you entrust your responsibility and share the keys. Not long after that came the cross, then the resurrection and the outpouring of the Spirit. From that point, everything changed.

Unlocking the Pathway

In today's turbulent spiritual atmospheres, the standard of Body maturity Paul outlined in his letter to the Ephesians is well within reach. The greatest hurdle is from within. It is the in-bred, short-sightedness in which the means becomes the end whereby leadership fails in its Kingdom function of serving, by taking on a life of its own.

During the course of the last generation, the rise of the parachurch movement, the influence and expansion of Christian media, distance learning and webinars, the mobilization of banners that bear on standards for legislation have all coincided with the acceleration of Body maturity, which in turn has met head-on, the inroads being made by darkness.

While the stakes are higher and the bar has been raised, God's keys of unlocking can be expected to retain their unstoppable potency. The standard of maturity and need for alignment – not unlike what David actuated in bringing all Israel together – is bedrock to all that lies ahead for the Lord's plans for the Church and for Israel. It begins with a faithful, strategically-poised remnant.

At the crux in this process is equipping the saints for the work of their callings. With the traction this yields, the mantle of David will be triggered in actuating unity for the revival-level manifested presence of God that mobilizes us as the community of believers needed for this hour.

During times of preparation, the focus will involve the infrastructures for timely life-training, from local congregations to Internet-based Kingdom-life programs to Bible schools and more, each preparing both leaders and the community for emerging as the Kingdom force that Jesus intended, to penetrate the darkness and draw all men to Himself.

"If you have run with footmen and they have wearied you, then how will you contend with horses. If in the land of peace in which you trusted they wearied you, then how will you do on the floodplain of the Jordan."
Jeremiah 12:5

CHAPTER 15

FEAR OF GOD

"Teach me your ways O Lord and I will walk in Your Truth. Unite my heart to fear Your Name." Psalm 86:11

During a recent mission to Benin, West Africa, we attended a traditional African Church wedding. It was a three hour service, unlike any wedding ceremony we have ever experienced in the West. The couple was exhorted on the foundations of their new relationship: in love, humility AND the fear of the Lord.

However, not only did the bride and groom take their vows of marriage, but the parents took vows to uphold the new relationship, in the fear of the Lord. Likewise, an older woman, a widow, considered wise in her ways was assigned to mentor the new wife during the first year of the marriage. There was more, but the thrust was that this new marriage became a responsibility of the community.

I later learned that this community, despite the odds during a major time of change, has not had one divorce in more than three decades.

Facing Times of Change

Since the 1970s, I have wielded a mantle in both business and ministry as a Kingdom marketplace pioneer. Repeatedly, this has involved assignments with those going through a significant time of change. Those I have served have ranged from ministries like CBN and Morris Cerullo to numerous well-known multinationals.

Working with leaders as well as with organizations, when change is underway and something new is being birthed, can take you into uncharted territory. It demands a hard look at what has been the mode of the past, in order to get the fix for the change required to embrace the future. It requires wisdom, flexibility and innovation.

For God's people, the fear of the Lord and humility are critical to entering times of change. Where leadership is involved, it will also involve honor. These factors are also at the heart of the igniters for those hungering for more of God, to see the consciousness of His presence manifest in genuine revival.

Facing change involves the need to prepare and to be prepared. The fear of the Lord is at the root of this ongoing need to prepare. It is the core to walking out a call of God. Walking with the Lord is progressive. It will always involve new dimensions.

From the Start

Proverbs tells us that the fear of the Lord is the beginning of wisdom. Yet, the fear of God is neither a gift nor a fruit of the Spirit, but a continuous choice foundational to our faith and bedrock to spiritual maturity and the knowledge of God.

Too often confused with self-control or a hyper-religious spirit, the fear of God is strengthened by the choices found only in a dimension "beyond ourselves." Over time, the hard choices become predispositions and a part of who we become in Him.

It was in late 1973, as a relatively young believer, that I left a military career to prepare for ministry at a Christian university. It was during those early days of walking with the Lord, that I first encountered the stiff realities of spiritual warfare with the death of one of our children. It was a shattering jolt. It challenged everything that lay before us in walking out our call of God.

Facing that reality left very little to lean on, other than the fear of the Lord. Friends offered words of comfort, yet very few actually achieved their intent. The only real comfort came from pressing through in prayer and God's presence.

From that time before the Lord, I sent a note to our closest friends. It expressed our choice, to trust the Lord. The focus of that note was from the response of Job in losing all that he had, including his children. In humility, Job fell on his face before God in repentance and worship.

"The Lord gave, and the Lord has taken away; blessed be the name of the Lord." Job 1:21

Walking out a call of God is a progressive thing. The comforts of this world entice, seduce and divide the mind. God had a higher dimension, something more, for Job.

Job was a man God loved. He did all the right things. Job was successful. He was a leader in the community. He was respected and honored by everyone in the area. Yet, Job fell short. In a day in time, everything changed for him. His losses included the honor that had come from his accomplishments. Job is a story of a dimension in God – that cannot be short-circuited – and the pathway to the protection and honor that only God can supply.

For Job to accomplish his destiny, he needed something more than the results of his own efforts. So it was that he went through a humbling that led to a new revelation of the Lord – and his knowledge of Him. Job learned that it is not what we can do for God. It is what we allow God to do through us.

The subtle difference of this truth is distinguished by the fear of God. When Job received the revelation that brought a much greater depth to his fear of God, not only was everything restored, but it was restored double. That included his receiving the honor that comes only to those who unequivocally fear the Lord.

The Standard

Psalm 15 is short, but pithy. It represents the standard for walking out a call of God. It is the standard for godly leadership and enduring relationships. It is the standard for protection in times of crisis, as well as the standard for revival.

Psalm 15 begins with the question of who is it who can abide and walk with God? It answers that it is the one who walks with integrity and works righteousness. Catch the phrase "WORKS righteousness." Righteousness here is referring to the Hebrew word "tz'dakah" which more correctly translated means righteous charity, a response to being a part of a community. It is something you do. It reflects being a doer of the Word.

This psalm goes on to describe the one who speaks truth within his own heart. Embracing truth and making it a part of one's life begins in the heart – the undivided heart. It describes a person who is true to their word and can be trusted. It goes on to say that the one who lives this standard does not slander nor exhibit any evil toward his neighbor.

It continues by noting that worldly success is not the standard. The one who has fallen into the trap of becoming a reprobate – of compromising – is worthy of being despised. However, those who FEAR THE LORD are to be HONORED. It mentions not taking advantage of the less fortunate, by charging interest or accepting a bribe against them. This psalm then concludes by proclaiming that those whose lives reflect these things will never be shaken.

At the foundation of the fear of the Lord are the components of humility and honor. The fear of God has many counterfeits designed to deceive even the elect. They range from pride, to idols in one's mind, to self-satisfaction, self-righteousness and self-justification, to the illusions that result from being double-minded. Only through humility and fear of the Lord will come the fullness of one's destiny in God.

"By humility and fear of the Lord are riches and honor and life."
Proverbs 22:4

Preparing for New Dimensions

In the opening scripture, the Psalmist reveals something very subtle for the one who seeks to walk in the ways of God. It involves a united heart. That means priority given to time spent with God, time seeking His heart.

Embracing oneness with God's heart calls for a united heart. That applies to both individuals and the body-corporate. Moreover, to release revival requires a united heart within the community of God's people.

Twice the book of James taps the observation of the "double-minded." In the first reference not only does the divided-mind not receive from God, it is described as unstable (James 1:8). In the second case (James 4:8), it lumps the double-minded together with sinners, with the admonition that heart-purification is needed for those whose attitudes and priorities are on both sides of the fence.

"Submit to God. Resist the devil and he will flee from you. Draw near to God and He will draw near to you. Cleanse your hands, you sinners; and purify your hearts, you double-minded." James 4:7-8

The purification needed from the snares of double-mindedness, more often than not will call for a strong dose of repentance and humility.

"Lament, mourn and weep. Let your laughter be turned to mourning and your joy to gloom. Humble yourselves in the sight of the Lord and He will lift you up." James 4:9

To the Finish

So, while the fear of the Lord is what lays the foundation for knowing the ways of God, it is also the thread of preparedness and maturity defining a stable and purposeful walk with Him. It is the factor that enables the finish to go well. As was seen with the African community, it is the glue for unity and stability. It establishes the wall of fire, the equalizer and protection for God's people that has no parallel.

It is the standard for enduring relationships, along with being the crux for God's criterion for leadership. Even more so, the fear of the Lord is bedrock for times of crisis and the igniter for what we describe as revival.

Carol and I came to faith during the vibrant days of the Jesus Movement. It was a time of great spiritual hunger that crossed the boundaries of sectarianism. It was a time of God's presence when people gathered together just to pray and seek God.

So it has been with those we work with in the persecuted church. The priority is God. Many of their leaders have had their faith forged in hard-labor prisons. They fear God more than what man can do to them. Their minds are focused and united. The double-minded, the masters of technique bypassing this critical dimension are fast to fall in this spiritual environment. The reality of God is gaining critical mass.

"Whether it is right in the sight of God to listen to you more than to God, you judge. For we cannot but speak the things which we have seen and heard." Acts 4:19-20

The world is looking for the reality of God being demonstrated – through His people. We've entered a time Jesus referred to in Matthew 24 as the "beginning of sorrows." We are approaching a time noted in Luke 21 when men's hearts will fail due to fear.

The determining factor for what's needed will not be a perfect doctrine, eloquent sermons or some super-elite band of hyper-religious. Nothing short of God's presence and power will suffice. The heart-stopping fear Jesus spoke of in Matthew 24 and Luke 21 is totally different from the fear of God. It is the response of those who do not know God and those whose hearts are divided toward him.

Before his ordeal, Job knew God and His ways, in his head. When he emerged, he truly knew God and His ways in his heart. The united heart changes everything.

115

"I have heard of You by the hearing of the ear, but now my eye sees You. Therefore I abhor myself, and repent in dust and ashes." Job 42:5-6

Critical Mass

God has called those known by His Name to be standard-bearers and agents of change. In today's chaotic and turbulent world, this task is going to take something more. We are to actuate a new dimension, the spiritual climate that establishes God's Kingdom rule.

The crucible to release God's presence and power is us. The antidote for the fear that causes hearts to fail is the fear of the Lord. The fear of the Lord is the awe, the reverence and total trust in the One who created the world and all who live in it. It is the oneness with Him whose Glory exceeds any dimension this world can offer. It is the humility that accepts the provision of His Truth with the honor due to His Name. It recognizes that, even with our best efforts, we fall short. His ways, His goodness, His wisdom are simply higher than our ways. He is the all-sufficient One.

"He who speaks from himself seeks his own glory, but He who seeks the glory of the One who sent Him is true, and no unrighteousness is in Him." John 7:18-19

The response, which will evolve into critical mass to be the catalyst, is the fear of the Lord, demonstrated through a people.

So it has been in the history of every revival, every move of God since the first-century church. When the fear of God reaches critical mass among the community of God's people, amazing, supernatural things start taking place. A genuine fear of God hungers for more of His presence. It produces steadfast prayer. Untiring prayer distinguished great revivalists such as John Wesley and Charles Finney, as well as moves of God such as the Moravians. It will be no different in this hour.

The Community Responsibility

Whether the purpose is fostering enduring relationships, establishing the standard for leadership, responding to times of change or crisis, or in serving as a catalyst for revival, the community of God's people is instrumental.

The responsibility undertaken by the African community to nurture the commitments of their newlyweds represents a significant example for our response to the times. The community of God's people is ultimately responsible for the infrastructure, preparedness and response needed to take God's people from one generation to another, in God.

"Keep your soul diligently so that you do not forget the things that your eyes have seen and they do not depart from your heart. Make them known to your children and your children's children." Deuteronomy 4:9

For more than three years, Jesus mentored his disciples. He unveiled God's ways so that they might truly know Him. Declaring that He was the way, the truth and the life, He opened the gates to release Kingdom power through His victory over death. He imparted the priorities of God's heart.

At the core of preparing this small band of those to whom He would entrust His mantle, was the fear of God. Once that took place, a change took place in His response to them. No longer did He refer to them as servants, but as friends. He had prepared them for change and once they got it, with a united heart and the fear of the Lord, He released them into their destiny.

"No longer do I call you servants, for a servant does not know what his master is doing; but I have called you friends." John 15:15

SECTION IV

THE EVIDENCE

CHAPTER 16

UNBROKEN

"Why do the nations rage and the people plot in vain? For the kings of the earth take their stand and the rulers take counsel together, against the Lord and against His Anointed, saying 'let us break their bonds in pieces and cast away their cords from us.'" Psalm 2:1-3

While having a great love for understanding the times and uncovering the depths in the knowledge of God, I continue to be astounded by the power implicit in the simple things that God has given us to confound the wise.

Few books I have read in recent years have had more of an impact on me than "Unbroken" by Laura Hillenbrand. It recounts the story of an Olympian runner, Louie Zamperini, who died in early 2014 at the age of 97. The story is uncommonly real and well-presented, written by the author of "Seabiscuit."

There's a message this story carries that relates to the times. It gives dramatic evidence of the reality of God in the affairs of men.

Having distinguished himself in the 1936 Olympics, Mr. Zamperini's chances at the gold in the 1940 Olympics were circumvented with the start of WWII. He became a bombardier and after many exploits in combat, was in a plane crash and lost in the Pacific. After an amazing survival story of 47 days drifting on a raft, he wound up as a Japanese POW.

During his captivity, he lived through two years of brutality and deprivation, many times believing, with cause, that he would not live another day. All this pervaded his upbeat, disciplined and resolute personality. Following the war, these emotional experiences began severely short-circuiting his future, until his amazing encounter with the Lord.

During the sixties, for two years I served as a combat Marine. During the many battles I experienced, I had more times than I care to recount, that I thought I was going to die. Not unlike Mr. Zamperini, I experienced a defiance in the face of death. These deeply personal experiences became the very bedrock by which the Lord revealed Himself to me, leading to my commitment as a Christian.

Those experiences also have become common ground with a number of the Christian leaders I work with in Vietnam who have spent two to three years in hard-labor prison camps for their faith, with far too many instances in not knowing if they would see the light of the next day, yet facing the ultimate test without wavering. Not unlike the Pacific POW camps of WWII, there were many who did not survive these internments.

In reading Mr. Zamperini's story, I found myself re-living many of my own close encounters with death. Despite a number of decorations for my actions in combat, I've never had the desire to share these "war stories" with others. There's something very personal, to a degree almost sacred, about encounters that cheat death.

The story of this extremely disciplined Olympian is emotional, as it relates the struggles he had upon his return to "normal" life after the war. Despite being a war hero, he employed masks to deal with the grip he was losing on regaining what he once had.

While understanding his trauma, I've personally never related very well to masks, phoniness or the superficial. My tolerance for these factors in Christian settings is even less because, in my view of things, they not only fall far short of God's standard and the expectations He has for those called by His name, they are snares that distance us from Him. Reality is defined by the One who created it. His reality is the standard to bring individuals and societies into the balance and healing sought by all.

Unreserved, God-focused commitment and disciplined, ongoing spiritual maintenance will nip even the most traumatic experiences in the bud. On the other hand, masks are what perpetuate and keep emotional baggage fed and alive.

However, there is another graphic illustration that the Zamperini story portrays. It is the picture of the systematic stripping of dignity, honor and hope that took place during his time in the prisoner of war camp. It is an apt picture of the evil behind the world's system, bent on squeezing the life out of the multitudes and separating people from the goodness of God.

Distortions of Reality

This dynamic triggers the unchecked illusions and distortions that operate all around us. It feeds into the aims of evil which wields the power of destruction and death. We see its operation in seats of power – as its cohorts attempt to define good as evil, and evil as good. Psalm 94:20 describes a throne of destruction which devises evil by law, which has absolutely no correlation to the goodness of God.

Those enticed with and who toy with special powers of death are bonding with and then establishing alliances with death. Death is at the very core of darkness. It is the last enemy to be abolished according to the Apostle Paul (1 Cor 15:26).

Jesus said even the very elect would face deceptive entrapments. The subtlety is that life and death are in the power of the tongue, with entice-ments that misuse the anointing and distort God's reality and power. The prophet wrote that: "Through deceit they refuse to know Me" (Jer 9:6). Only God, can remedy the entangled webs of evil designed to ensnare and bring down even those of an upright heart. Humility and fear of the Lord are the antidotes. Whereas pride and the ambitious pursuit of power will corrupt, the truly humble and contrite of spirit will never be turned away.

In short, as individuals known by His name, we are called to bless and not curse, to give life and not death. Jesus instructed us to bless even our enemies. The calling of Abraham explains that this is God's purview alone. Indeed, God will bless those who bless His own, but will also curse those who try to curse those known by His name.

Defilements

Distortions of reality and alliances with death have resulted in a world rampant with spiritual defilements. Death has embedded itself in the cultures of the world and the traditions of men, albeit superstitions, to the extent that they are accepted and embraced as normal. Ever see a thirteenth floor on elevator stops of a tall building?

What took place in the Japanese POW camp with Louie Zamperini is the manifestation of evil resident in the world. It parallels what those I've already mentioned, in being persecuted for their faith have gone through. The evil one specializes in pathways of defilements that lead to brokenness.

King David, after his fall, understood the dynamics that God's people have to contend with. They involve not only sin, but the defilements, cre-ated by the cultural iniquities, which combine in their intent to divert and crush the progress of good. In Psalm 51 David cries out to the Lord to be washed from those iniquities which culturally crowd the righteous as snares and triggers of sin. Many have been the times I have returned from ministering overseas and penetrating the lairs of darkness only to feel an overwhelming need for a "spiritual bath." These are the times in which priority needs to be given to getting alone with the Lord with immersions in His presence and truth.

God's presence and truth cleanses and restores. Yet this process demands a right heart, a heart of humility and a strong, continual dose of the fear of the Lord.

"Wash me from my iniquity and cleanse me from my sin. You desire truth in the inward parts and in the hidden part You will make me to know wisdom. Purge me with hyssop, and I shall be clean. . . . Create in me a clean heart, O God, and renew a steadfast spirit within me. Do not cast me away from Your presence. Restore to me the joy of Your salvation. Then I will teach transgressors Your ways, and sinners shall be converted to You." From Psalm 51:2-13

Response to the Counterfeit: The Design by God

The story of Louie Zamperini is a story of the colliding – between a life held in the bondage of masks and the superficial – and the reality that only God can provide and bring into wholeness. It is a story of facing your fears. It is a story of becoming a true God-pleaser and embracing reality.

We live in a world of illusions. What we refer to as smoking mirrors is employed at the highest levels. The perception has been confused with the reality. Masks define identities. Superficialities drive priorities. Leadership is mistaken for who is in charge.

Jesus came to reset the way we look at things. He came to unmask the counterfeit. He unveiled the realities, which redefine the priorities. There's a major difference between brokenness and humility. Humility is the process of taking the steps to remove the masks and face the fears that the evil one uses in paths to brokenness.

In this upside-down world, the illusions warp true reality with the distortions intent on seducing the multitudes into pathways of destruction. Yet, from the beginning, God has had a design for His people.

Jesus described this design and raised the bar for what God gave to His covenant people. At its core is the purpose, which God gave to Abraham in calling him out of the world, that he might "be blessed to be a blessing." The model of economic community with God at the helm also came from the way Abraham and then Moses organized community, which in effect, is as a light shining on a hill. He provided the foundations to operate as a culture within a culture, one that makes a difference.

God's design defines the pathway defining our lives. It is more, much more, than just the idle talk and the clutter which overshadows the world around us. This design is a paradox to the way the world thinks and perceives the realities. It is the way of the Kingdom.

God's design is the pathway that leads to Life, not a counterfeit or distorted illusion, but rather true Life. Jesus made it plain that it is a narrow and difficult path. There is a simplicity in entering its gates, but a steadfast resolve that is needed to overcome the seductive hurdles to maintain the focus and stay the course.

The reality is that within the world in which we live, what we are traversing is a narrow corridor between Life and death. Yet death and the fear of death, when the path is maintained according to God's design, has no grip on us. The Kingdom is distinguished by a simple strategy: the application of righteous power in corrupt settings.

Those who have been delivered from the occult recognize the realities between Life and death. At the crux of the occult are flirtations and manipulations with death. Evil is a magnet for death. So is pride, especially the pride behind quests for power. Destruction and poverty result when death rules.

"Can a throne of destruction be allied with You, one which devises mischief by decree? They band themselves together against the life of the righteous, and condemn the innocent to death." Psalm 94:20-21

The story of Louie Zamperini illustrates how people, believers and non-believers alike, put God in a box. They establish their own order of illusions. They mask the realities of life with superficialities. Then there comes a time when the order established by human limitations falls short. Surviving both the plane crash and then the 47 days on a raft was a jolt to the former priorities of Mr. Zamperini's life.

The Fear of the Lord

Whether brokenness is the result of blindness created by prideful superficialities or circumstances beyond ones control or both, the Lord embraces such ones, who if they maintain the focus of genuine humility, He will then make whole.

"By humility and fear of the Lord are riches and honor and life." Proverbs 22:4

The combination of humility and true fear of the Lord equip us to face the ultimate tests. Those I've worked with in Vietnam who were imprisoned for their faith understand this reality. For that reason, and having been refined by such fires, they are steadfast and unbroken. Yet without the dimensions of the fear of the Lord and genuine humility, the pathway leads to simply becoming "full of ourselves."

A consciousness of God's presence is evident among these former "prisoners for the Lord." It is tangible. So likewise is the anointing that defines their perspectives and priorities. It is not surprising that the fruit from their efforts represent the seedbeds for revival and the sparks that penetrate the darkness that is changing the spiritual climates of their domains.

The fear of the Lord is at the crux of being whole. Alternately, at the core of stumbling within Christian circles, even leadership circles, are the masks and superficialities that distort true identities and open the door for the defilements designed to short-circuit God-designed destinies

The psalmist got it. He wrote in Psalm 23 that the Lord restores our soul and leads us in a pathway of righteousness. Then even when we walk through the valley of the shadow of death that we will fear no evil – for the Lord will be with us. The Lord will comfort us. He will also prepare a table before us in the presence of our enemies. In short, we can expect the demonstration of God's reality on our behalf, even as darkness covers the earth. It is then that we will shine the brightest.

"Arise, shine for your light has come and the glory of the Lord has risen upon you. For darkness will cover the earth and deep darkness the people. But the Lord will arise over you and His glory will be seen upon you. Gentiles shall come to your light and kings to the brightness of your rising." Isaiah 60:1-3

CHAPTER 17

HIDDEN WISDOM

"Wisdom is better than might, although a poor man's wisdom is despised and his words not heeded. The words of the wise, spoken quietly, should be heard, rather than the shout of those who rule among fools."
Ecclesiastes 9:16-17

The Word of God is a treasure trove of the wisdom for life, together with the principles needed for the community of God's people to live out their destinies, according to His ways. Solomon was anointed with extraordinary wisdom. Yet, in all his observations (Eccl 3:11), he was quick to note that the extents and depths of God were beyond the best of our human capacities.

Among his reflections in Ecclesiastes is the story of a small community that was attacked by a numerically superior force (Eccl 9:14-16). Within that city was a poor man who possessed the wisdom that saved the city. Yet, once the status quo was restored, no one remembered him.

Repeatedly Solomon points to truths reflecting the need for the practical, often hidden wisdom to reorient our distorted, short-sighted view and value of things. He notes that a living dog is better than a dead lion and that a dead fly can cause the perfumer's ointment to putrefy and smell vile.

Solomon also discerns (Eccl 9:18) that while wisdom can prove mightier than weapons of war, one sinner can destroy inherent good. So it was with the story of the poor, wise man, who saved the city. The wisdom of the poor man who saved the city did not conform to the prevailing popular perception of things.

God's available wisdom too often can be constrained and overshadowed by distorted prisms and be sought from the wrong places.

The Right Thing the Wrong Way

Jacob went through many years of hardship by reaching for the right thing the wrong way.

While his clever deceits pushed the envelope, he faced setbacks because there was always someone a little more clever than he was. Despite his dramatic, life-changing encounter with the Angel of the Lord, as he finally acknowledged that he was in over his head, when faced with reuniting with Esau, his ways influenced and were passed on to his sons.

The sons of Jacob defiled what God intended for their generational blessing and destiny, when deceitfully they took things into their own hands over the matter of their sister Dinah and Shechem.

The story of Joseph is one of God's anticipatory redemption of the calling that flowed from his great-grandfather Abraham. It was marked by hidden wisdom, the prophetic wisdom that God invested in Joseph. However, at its start, within his own household, this wisdom was despised and resented by all, except Jacob.

In reading the history of God's people, from generation to generation, it has followed the same sequence. God demonstrates His power and blessing with a generation that finally "gets it" and establishes something eternal, only to have it marginalized, with the "God-essence" squeezed out with a misguided, but prevailing "conventional," often contemporary wisdom.

What seems to result is short-sighted, as the real significance of what God has done succumbs to defilements and myopic diminishments. When deliverance comes through "hidden" wisdom, the reality is that it had already been evidenced in the prior generations. The cycle of recovery comes through a generation getting "beyond themselves," in repentant humility, in their quest for that "something more" dimension in God.

The Cultural Threshold

There is a threshold that has been sought by cultures and generations. It is the threshold that taps the resources of God's glory. It is the chasm that is bridged when the limitations of the natural are superseded by the supernatural.

"The race is not to the swift, nor the battle to the strong, neither is bread to the wise nor riches to men of intelligence and understanding, nor favor to men of skill." Ecclessiates 9:11

When released, dramatic change results. No power on earth can stand against it. Yet, not unlike the time of the tower of Babel, cultures and generations possess a power, blinded against God that transcends the sum of it parts.

This power ties into the dynamic of the tree of knowledge that was perverted in the garden. Counterfeits have since abounded. It is why God told Abraham to leave his family and the country of Ur, the land of the Chaldeans where sorcery had its roots.

God's glory and the release of His hidden wisdom will not abide or compromise with either the occult or pop wisdom. It operates on a spiritual level far beyond the counterfeits and illusions of a watered-down status quo. This threshold must be overcome in God to see the true reality of God operating. When this takes place, it releases what we call revival or the ongoing manifest Presence of God among a people.

In his interactions with the rulers of the lands where sorcery dominated, Abraham began being recognized as the man with a quietness of wisdom that commanded the respect of having as its source, the one true God. When a culture, religion or the occult faces the purity of God, Light will always dispel darkness.

Throughout the history of God's people, it has always been a choice of the real or the counterfeit.

The Source of Blindness

To understand the gap to be bridged, we need to understand the biblical concept of iniquities. While some simply count iniquities as sin, which they are, they are more than that. Some also view iniquities as generational sins, which indeed they are.

However, again and again, the context of iniquities is cultural. Iniquities are something deeper and ingrained in the traditions of men, taken on and passed on not only by a generation, but by a culture of people.

Iniquities are the hidden, often deemed acceptable sins of a people. The story of the sons of Jacob and their response to Shechem and their sister Dinah is a story of these sons embracing the conniving, deceitful iniquities of their father.

Yet in Micah 7:19 the Word of God tells us that God will "subdue" our iniquities. It will come from our pure, humble response and grasp of His presence.

The fine line is in closing the door to iniquities, while sinking deep roots of our cultural identities – in God.

"You shall teach these things diligently to your children, and shall talk of them when you sit in your house, when you walk by the way, when you lie down, and when you rise up." Deuteronomy 6:7

Iniquities are in essence hidden masks. They replace the gaps of our understanding of the ways of God with distorted human understanding. They become snares and hurdles to the pure presence of God. Examples of iniquities impeding the wisdom that only God can provide are the cleverness, conniving, pretense and limitations of human reasoning. Their subtle roots are removed only by the diligent mix of seeking God as first priority and repentance.

The roots of iniquities are found in the subtleties of pride. It is why the Word of God places so much importance on humility. Humility is the cloak needed for a generation to overcome the transgressions that have become the established way around them.

Throughout Proverbs we are warned about pride. Prideful enlargement is equated with death by Habakkuk (Hab 2:5). While the Lord is the God of increase, the right thing done the wrong way is wrong. Likewise, Samuel rebuked Saul with the observation that stubbornness is as the sin of witchcraft. In like fashion, Jesus again and again told his followers to "fear not." Each of these factors are subtle, generally condoned behaviors that mask the operation of the pure, "hidden" wisdom reflected by the poor man, which is readily available, but too often remains dormant in the Word of Truth.

The Wellspring

There are factors that accelerate the process by which a generation of God's people peel back and grasp the wisdom required for times of change. It begins with recognizing the need. The process both begins and advances by tapping and becoming immersed in the Wellspring.

When God's people come together in unity and humility, seeking the Lord, then revelation is imparted. With Solomon's insight of there being nothing new under the sun, what is fresh and new for the needs of a generation is in reality ancient wisdom, hidden in God's Word.

"Teachers who have been instructed in the Kingdom are like the owner of a house who brings out of his storeroom new treasures as well as old." Matthew 13:52

Paul wrote the Colossians (2:9) that in Jesus is the embodiment, the fullness of the Godhead. In Him are the depths of the wisdom that Solomon, despite all his own extensive anointing in wisdom, recognized as the wellspring of wisdom that is beyond any human capacity. Jesus is the Source.

Tapping the Source

Jesus made it very clear that a key role of the Holy Spirit is to impart truth. Jesus told His followers that when the Holy Spirit came, He would guide us into truth (John 16:13).

The acceleration of this process of tapping the hidden wisdom that releases God's supernatural into otherwise impossible situations will combine an unequivocal cultural identity in God, a clear grasp of the cause from God's heart, a mobilized following, embracing the Holy Spirit as teacher, and a bedrock priority to our faith.

Cultural Identity. From the beginning, God's people have served as a distinct culture within the surrounding cultures. Their identity has been as a people of God. This is the observation that Jesus made in John 17 when He said we would be in the world, but not of the world. We are citizens of God's Kingdom and God's ambassadors demonstrating His reality and life to a world without hope.

Grasp of the Cause. God has always intended those who are known by His Name to be a people of influence, bearing the mantle of Abraham, to be blessed to be a blessing. God's priorities and focus will result when our hearts become truly aligned with His heart. That means time spent with Him and spiritual maintenance.

We are people of truth, bearing witness to the standard of truth established by the One who is the source of truth. We are catalysts changing the spiritual climate in our sphere, penetrating the darkness with His light. This is the driving purpose for both individuals and the community of His people.

Mobilized Following. The role of leadership is mobilizing God's people in their life-purpose to make a difference in the surrounding society. One of the most subtle spiritual immobilizers has been the dichotomy between the sacred and the secular whereby the success of spiritual leaders is judged by the ability to raise money. Fund-raising and increase may be involved, but the goal is not money, it's the by-product. Nor is the primary goal congregational membership or attendance at services, but rather the mobilization and equipping of every true believer into God's specific calling on their lives.

The Holy Spirit as Teacher. The only way every believer can be activated and guided into the fullness of their purpose is by introducing them to a proactive prayer life and the role of the Holy Spirit as their Teacher, Who guides them into the truths bearing on their life-purpose.

The Priority of Faith. For the most part, the way of the Kingdom is a paradox to the way the world normally operates. Bedrock to our faith is the fine line between recognizing that it is not what we can do for God, but rather what we allow Him to do through us. That truth, together with accessing God's hidden wisdom, rests on a humility, which is required to be truly led by Spirit, rather than becoming ambitious zealots whose efforts are the result of human confidence and achievement.

The alignment of these factors, both individually and as a community, will open the gates into the secret place of His presence. They become the catalyst for the release of God's manifest presence. From that will flow the hidden wisdom from above, against which no other power can stand.

The Secret Place

I've long recognized this type of resolute identity with those who have found that "secret place" of regularly abiding in God's presence. Leaders I've worked with in persecuted nations who have spent time in prison for their faith have found that secret place. It is clearly not a matter of "what you know," but rather "Who you regularly abide with."

Joseph found that secret place in God as a slave and then, due to no fault of his own, experienced spiritual backlash and became a prisoner. Having lost his family and his freedom when enslaved in Egypt, Joseph never had an issue with his identity. It was recognized by all those around him. Everyone saw that God was with him and that he extended the blessing of God to those he served (Gen 39:2-4), making all that he did to prosper. His identity was firmly established in God. He operated as a culture within a culture.

Despite Joseph's lowly position as a slave and then prisoner, an authority and influence flowed from his identity, his faith and his purpose in God. It flowed from the hidden wisdom that came from the secret place of God's presence, a place that Joseph learned to abide in and use as the navigator through the challenging corridors in his journey to God's place of opportunity and destiny. Pure faith and humility will always close the gap and open the gates into God-opportunities.

"He who speaks from his own self seeks his own glory, but he who seeks the glory of Him who sent him is true and no unrighteousness dwells in him." John 7:18

CHAPTER 18

DOING GOOD

"So then, while we have opportunity, let us do good to all men, especially to those who are of the household of faith." Galatians 6:10

As a Body, we tend to get myopic. That's not something new. It's a plague that has been grappled with since there has been a household of faith. It's why there are so many groupings and divides within those who bear His Name.

This myopia has made its mark following every biblical and post-biblical revival over the centuries. Genuine spiritual renewals have life-cycles in *the dynamic of God's manifested presence* displacing evil. The reality-of-God imparted is so far beyond human grasp that anything short of the anointing, designed to prolong its potency, just tends to weaken and diminish the results. So over time, the progressive, imperfect blending of the natural and impure short-circuits the supernatural.

Revivals are times when God's manifest presence expands and illuminates our horizons. Revivals create movements that change things. Historically though, movements have digressed into becoming institutionalized. In that process the fire and power fade. This is by no means a swipe at institutions, but rather a call to give focus to what is truly important in this process: knowing Him and being a light to those around us. It's the reason why we need to overcompensate with listening hearts as different segments of the Body interact. No one group has a pure grasp, not to speak of the capacity, for the total picture.

In further illustrating this myopia, doctrine is the means rather than the end. When we stand before the Lord on that final day, we're not going to be examined on the basis of doctrine, but rather our heart responses to

God and those around us and the difference our lives have made. That also is not a swipe against sound doctrine. Rather, it is to recognize the reality of the myopia – which has a long track record of missing the forest for the trees – in order to give focus to reaching for what is most important.

Sound doctrine serves the purpose of establishing our identity in Him and the character to walk out the purpose of a life of faith: doing good. That's not the premise of salvation, but rather the result of it.

Jesus punctuated this significant distinction, based not on our limited perceptions of righteousness, but instead on the evidence reflected by the consistency of our practices, as demonstrators of the truth we claim to believe.

"For everyone practicing evil hates the light and does not come to the light, lest his deeds be exposed. But he who DOES THE TRUTH comes to the light, that his deeds may be clearly seen, that they have been done in God." John 3:19-21

All of which brings us to the point made by Paul in the opening scripture. In the mandate to "do good," first priority is to be given to the household of faith.

Raising the Bar

Jesus came to raise the bar. Some within the Body have concluded that Jesus came to establish a new religion. Others have digressed into the same trap of elitism that snared the Pharisees, only with a Christian spin to it. Each is equally myopic.

Jesus made it very clear that He came not to destroy the law and the prophets, but to bring fulfillment to that foundation. He went to the degree of saying that whoever broke one of the lesser parts of the law, the Torah AND taught others to do likewise, that they would be deemed least in the Kingdom. He didn't say they would be expelled, He said their impact would be diminished to where they would be considered among the least.

There's something about these foundations that Jesus never intended to be excluded. It's because truth can be overshadowed by short-sighted precepts. Watering down dilutes. Jesus said: "He who is faithful in what is least, is faithful also in much."

That's why we need to extract ourselves from the myopia and start reaching for the big-picture. Jesus always clarified and gave focus to central issues and the strategic. His response to the Pharisee who asked Him

135

what was most important (Matt 22:39) was to "Love the Lord your God with all your heart and your neighbor as your self."

To the rich young ruler's query, Jesus first advised him (Matt 19:17-21) not to murder, commit adultery, steal, or bear false witness – and to honor his parents and love his neighbors as himself. Self-righteously, the rich young man then asked what he lacked, since he met each of these criteria. Jesus' response, "if he truly wanted to be perfect," was to divest his assets and give them to the poor and then follow Him.

Jesus raised the bar. For each one Jesus called, it involved a step beyond themselves. Doctrines and followings have resulted from focus given to the uniqueness of the criterion for different callings. Yet, it wasn't the same for each. The calling of Peter was very different from the calling of Nathaniel, as it was from the calling of Levi.

For each, it was very personal. The key was in the reorientation, in response to truth. and with that, in the walk that followed.

The significance is in the walk, not the criteria of the calling. For some, like Peter, it took longer than others. But then, perhaps it was because the bar was higher for his calling. Consistently, since His earthly ministry, Jesus has pulled people out of their short-sighted muck and set them on a big-picture course to make a difference. It is a course of "doing good" with a process that has as much significance as the ends.

"If you are presenting your offering at the altar and remember that your brother has something against you, then go, be reconciled to your brother, before presenting your gift." Matthew 5:23, 24

The Challenge
Carol and I came to faith during a time of God-birthed revival. We were drawn and greatly impacted by what we saw operating in the walk of certain believers. We saw the reality of God being demonstrated. It was beyond the ordinary. It tied back to a leader who was nurturing God's blueprint for a group of spiritually hungry pilgrims.

Over time, the growth of this man's effort resulted in new leaders being brought in to work with him. Their approach was not as far-sighted and innovative as what the founder had established. Division resulted that ultimately scattered the foundational work. The confusion and disarray resulted in many casualties among those who had been in the process of being helped.

Another example took place in a completely different time frame in another part of the world. The founder of a far-sighted work brought much benefit to the entire household of faith in this area. However, a member of his board became offended. Despite public overtures, the result was the offense becoming a seedbed taken up by others in the leadership. Deceit ran rampant and eventually the founder was squeezed out. The short story is that the "ousters" failed in their attempt to replicate what had been established and the entire effort floundered and was shut down.

Many other examples of misuses of authority, presumption, blind-spots and misguided tongues mark short-sighted spiritual conditions that create fleshly responses to and within otherwise God-birthed agendas and movements. Peter advised us to be wary of our adversary the devil. We indeed live in a fallen world.

Misguided Influence

On the other hand, James warned that teachers would be held to a higher standard and judged more strictly. So it is with those in leadership. The tripping point bearing myopic ripples underscoring this warning is with the factor of community influence.

The tendency is to bypass the standard for biblical community and God's blueprint for His followers, by myopically making an idol of the community/ ministry effort rather than it being the platform for nurturing and serving.

God's design for biblical community is as a safe place. It's a place where the diversity of gifts and mantles within its members can flow, grow, give benefit to one another and be a blessing to all exposed to it. Instead, it too often can be a war zone. Far too often, that is how the world sees us as a people of God: for the differences, enmities and division.

Jesus said we would know "them" by their fruits. The fruits from the founders of these two examples above fit the criteria Jesus spoke of in being a light on a hill that could not be hidden. However, the fruit for those whose efforts brought down their works – are the casualties and those who never got helped by the imperfect, although anointed efforts of the founders.

Whenever the fruit involves a history of casualties created by those whose ends seem to justify short-sighted means, if correction is not prompt, the result will be judgment. It bears on the myopia, the maturity and the maintenance required for those wielding the mantles of leader-ship. Within the crucible, even among the elite in Jewish circles, is Jacob's corner-cutting iniquity and Ephraim's enmity.

"Ephraim was called as a watchman and prophet to the surrounding nations; but has become a fowler's snare in all his ways. There is enmity, hostility, and persecution in the house of his God." Hosea 9:8

Similarly, throughout the household of faith, are the misguided crusaders who would tear down established works for flaws and premature judgments, driven by myopic blind spots, which overshadow the good. Hypocrisy defiles the standard and the process.

Defining the Focus
Jesus said (Mark 9:49): "Everyone will be seasoned with fire and every sacrifice will be seasoned with salt."

This statement follows Jesus' comment (v 42) that whoever causes one of these little ones to stumble, it would be better if a millstone was hung around his neck and he was cast into the sea. That's pretty strong.

Matthew has a parallel reference to this truth (Matt 18:6,7). It highlights the OFFENSES of causing ones less mature, under one's influence, to stumble. Jesus' reference to offenses wasn't about hurt feelings. He was talking about short-sighted applications of power and truth. Jesus was pointing to those whose blind-spots or immaturity result in misguided use of their authority and influence, which creates casualties among those under their authority.

The answer is in the application of the truth, in the salting, which preserves and gives flavor and life to the walk and to the work. Jesus' solution doesn't pamper. He says if your hand causes you to sin, then cut it off. If it's your eye, then pluck it out. He was drawing from Isaiah 33:15, a truth which illustrates a standard in which one keeps his hands from taking bribes and his eyes from considering evil. It's about relationships and honor.

It emphasizes the importance and assurance of a trustworthy relational foundation that reflects *the seasoning needed to operate in peace toward one another.*

"Have salt in yourselves and peace with one another." Mark 9:50

One of the most profound doctrinal statements I've yet to hear is: "God is a good God and the devil is a bad devil." Trust is a mark in the dividing line between good and evil. Jesus raised the bar so that the household of faith would uphold that standard and become that "city set on a hill that cannot be hidden."

The Apostle James strongly emphasizes holding to the standard as DOERS of the Word. The admonition is to make it a lifestyle.

"Prove yourselves to be doers of the Word and not merely hearers, who deceive themselves." James 1:22

Jesus points to the big-picture with the priority He calls on to be given to the stewardship of preparation and doing.

"Who then is that faithful and wise steward, whom his master will make ruler over his household, to give them their portion in due season? Blessed is that servant whom his master will find so DOING when he comes. Truly, I say to you that he will make him ruler over all that he has. But the one who knew his master's will, and did not prepare himself or do according to his will, shall be beaten with many stripes." Luke 12:42-45

The big picture purpose will become clearer as we get our interim priorities aligned. Then God's judgment against evil will trigger the gates to His glory being manifested within the household of faith.

"Lift up your heads, O gates, and be lifted up, O ancient doors, that the King of glory may come in! Who is the King of glory? The Lord strong and mighty, the Lord mighty in battle. Lift up your heads, O gates, and lift them up, O ancient doors, that the King of glory may come in! Who is the King of glory? The Lord of hosts, You are the King of glory." Psalm 24:6-10.

The world sees beyond the press releases and promotional spins given by the household of faith. The world is looking for the reality of God. The process, as a people – not the end – is our witness. That is why revival is so significant. God's presence is a consuming fire. It is the irresistible draw that cuts past the superficial and phony and gives focus to what matters and what is real.

For those awash in the evil and turbulence taking place in the world today, we – the household of faith – are the signposts and lifeboats. People will be drawn by what they see operating within our ranks. When we get the "doing good" right, THEN the reality of God is demonstrated, which draws the world like a magnet.

The big picture is in doing good, but getting it right first within the household of faith.

"So, let your light shine before men, that they may see your GOOD WORKS and glorify your Father in heaven." Matthew 5:16

CHAPTER 19

THE CREATIVE PATH

"God thunders with His majestic voice, doing great things which we cannot comprehend. For by Him all things were created that are in heaven and on earth, visible and invisible, whether thrones or dominions or principalities or power." Job 37:5, Col 1:16

In God's nature is found a basis from which to think, to act and prioritize the decisions of life. It is a creative path. Moses tapped its parameters. So did Joseph and Daniel and David. For each, it changed everything and made them heroes of faith. Jesus then added substance to this framework and raised the bar. At its foundation is the way of the Kingdom.

It begins by knowing the One who is the Creator, the One who transcends time and our limited perspectives of the realities around us. In knowing the Lord, we begin uncovering what we refer to as His truth, His nature and His ways. Then as we discipline ourselves to know Him according to His ways, our thoughts and attitudes begin to be aligned with His.

It is THEN that the Lord will allow us into His inner sanctum and expose us to the unlimited, creative dimensions of His nature.

The Glory of His Presence

Solomon inferred that these unlimited dimensions of God were the stuff of kings (Prov 25:3). No doubt a king's perspective, as Solomon bore the responsibility of spiritually guiding those for whom he was accountable.

There's no question that these dimensions of God are beyond the ordinary thresholds of how most people are wired to think and act. Paul described these unlimited facets of His presence as the riches of God's glory. Jesus advanced this reality by admonishing His followers to seek the oneness of abiding – in Him.

In His presence is a glory to be partaken when our interactions with Him are pure. The heart of God desires a people willing to transcend the boundaries of human limitations and in truth, meekness and righteousness (Ps 45:4), to share in these dimensions with Him.

In approaching these boundless dimensions of His nature, there is a pathway that uncovers, engenders and releases the creative. Discerning the voice of the Lord is the gateway. This gateway leads to the discovery of much more.

In heeding his call as prophet, Isaiah was given an assignment that addressed the dullness and desolation that results from NOT hearing the voice of the Lord (Isa 6:9). Isaiah went on to make it plain that God's ways are simply higher than ours and beyond our normal comprehension (Isa 55:9).

Similarly, God's nature is to bring increase. From God's promise to Abraham for descendents beyond his ability to number, to Jesus' parable of the talents, God's expectation for good stewards is in bringing increase.

As God's very nature is creative, with His Spirit within us, we have the means to go beyond the boundaries of our human limitations and what we, in the natural, perceive and "know." When our way is stymied, a single God-thought can be the release.

New Mind-Sets

With God at the center, this unfolding path holds the potential of being illuminated by our mind-sets, the way we think. While the precepts of men tends to impede progress, the way of the Kingdom, facilitates release.

The Catalyst of Vision. When God told Abraham to gaze at the heavens, telling him his descendents would be as numerous as the stars, He was casting vision. He had already told Abraham that He was his shield, his exceeding great reward. He wanted Abraham to visualize that His promises far exceeded Abraham's ability to grasp them. Abraham's response was to believe God which pleased God greatly. The faith-response of vision is the igniter to bringing that which is not into being, of creating something out of nothing, through God.

Investigative-Approach. Proverbs suggests that the prudent man is cautious and considers well his steps (Prov 14:15). That caution is not in believing God, but in the steps that need to be taken. That suggests diligence in doing our homework. It means that there is wisdom in asking questions and investigating a matter thoroughly, as there will always be something hidden or not obvious to be uncovered and considered. That's why it is important to ask the right questions and push the envelope in considering alternatives.

Imagination. There is an untapped potential triggered by our imaginations. Imagining is the ability to form new images and concepts in our minds. Our imaginations actuate the bridge between the natural and spiritual worlds, between vision and reality. With faith in God, it carries untapped potential. Jesus noted that one can be guilty of negative things entertained in their imaginations. Likewise, one's imagination gives shape to their vision. It's a vital ingredient for acting in faith.

The Process of Planning. Planning and goal-setting is a means of identifying the steps needed to bring vision into reality. It is a process of evaluating the response to alternatives. Planning is continuous. It is a process of evaluating things that recognizes there is always something more. Cooperative planning with the Holy Spirit gives the Lord opportunity to add that expanded dimension of His thoughts into the process of establishing vision, goals and strategies.

Strategy. Good strategy is the purpose of good planning. Mapping out the steps for the pathway gives shape to maximizing opportunity and bringing increase. While good strategy is sought, the higher dimensions of God's nature elevate the standard much more than just good ideas. The need is the prophetic dimensions of God-ideas. This is what set Joseph apart in the eyes of Pharaoh and resulted in his promotion. Joseph did more than just accurately interpret Pharaoh's dreams. He mapped out a strategy. Pharaoh recognized the prophetic wisdom resident within Joseph as coming from God.

Excellence. Daniel was described as ten times better than any of the advisors of the king's court around him. Excellence involves becoming expert in something, to the degree that whatever the developed gift, it goes beyond that of the standard held by most others.

The Strategy of Faith and Prayer
Whereas wisdom is the application of God's principles, creativity is the discovery and application of bringing the invisible world into

the visible one. God's strategy to bring this about is through faith and prayerful, interactive time in His presence.

New mind-sets represent a way of viewing things and problem solving. The process of employing these factors generates insights that lead to creative discovery.

That's how it operates on an individual level. Yet, God's design for biblical community is the value-added of the creative dynamic available through God. It represents a safe-place fostering these higher dimensions of God. Incorporated in its design is to build from generation to generation. It demonstrates the reality of God through a people. It utilizes a model dating back to Abraham.

From age to age, biblical community has engendered consistent success despite adversities and backlash that God's chosen have experienced from the very different, but dominant cultures of which they have been a part. There are specific factors bearing on the strategy of community with which this pathway operates.

The Strategy of Community

Over the millennia the Jewish people not only have succeeded in retaining their cultural identity, but with disproportionate achievement have served as catalysts and influencers to the civilizations that would rise and fall around them, like the Greeks, the Romans, the Assyrians, the Ottomans, the Babylonians and on and on.

Historically, in civilizations without a middle class, the Jewish people have served that function, as merchants and bankers and people of business. They have been advisors to kings, rulers and leaders and financed national agendas in the societies in which they lived.

Yet, as a people, Jews have been distinctive. As a people, they have released nuggets of wisdom from the roots of their faith-culture that have impacted the foundations: economically, governmentally, judicially, and morally, for what is now considered as the good and enduring virtues of Western civilization.

Today, despite being less than a quarter of one percent of the world's population, since 1950, Jews have been the recipients of 27 percent of the Nobel prizes awarded. Studies such as "The Golden Age of Jewish Achievement" and "Startup Nation" attest to their contributions, which statisticians would view as "beyond chance expectation."

In short, the means by which Jews have tapped the creative has resulted in them outliving, as a people, the civilizations of which they have been a part.

Pertinent Ancient Wisdom

Identity. At the foundation of Jewish culture is their identity. They hold to the belief of being a prophetic people of God whose ways were outlined by Moses, the prophets and their forefather Abraham, as they have been blessed to be a blessing. They have resisted assimilation as, from age to age, they have maintained their unique identity as a culture within a culture.

Entrepreneurship. True entrepreneurship is by definition creative. Nurturing entrepreneurship changes the status quo and provokes opportunity. It fosters a creativity that builds from the bottom up. Former Cambridge professor, entrepreneurial expert and author, Bill Bolton (with John Thompson, "Entrepreneurs, Talent, Temperament, Technique"), stresses the importance of the creative and innovative dimensions which drive economic opportunity and the dynamic of entrepreneurship.

Trust Society. From the days of Moses, Jewish beliefs nurture the dynamic of community as much or more than any other culture; but with the approach of being a trust society. A highly respected social economist has uncovered some unique insights into these issues in his examination of economies and cultures in "Trust: Social Virtues and the Creation of Prosperity."

Francis Fukuyama contends that social capital is as important as physical capital. Yet, only societies with a high degree of social trust will create the foundations needed for the large-scale business organizations that compete in today's global economy. However, large-scale organizations are only a part of the equation as enduring prosperity for community flows first from the bottom-up entrepreneurially.

Opportunity Enablers. Within the Jewish community, there is a nurturing that is the natural order of things. The more successful advise those entering new arenas. The older, more experienced help those who are younger. Mentoring benefits all as the diversity of gifts blend together for the common good and opportunity is enabled.

Self-Sufficiency. Within this context, when adhering to these standards, the Jewish people operate in a self-regulated, self-sufficiency within their communities. They nurture the type of stewardship that serves and reflects excellence. Their forefather Abraham began his adventurous sojourn with God by being told that as God blessed him, that through his descendents, then that blessing of God would be extended to all the families of the earth. That requires a unique form of leadership.

Leadership. The Jewish brand of leadership has the distinction of operating best through influence and service. As a people, Jews lead by example. Jews are disciplined and are willing to pay the cost to live at a higher standard, to sacrifice for the future of their people.

Moral Standards. Jews as a people of God uphold a high moral standard as a society. Their distinctive identity upholds the standards of community, entrepreneurship, innovation, excellence and industriousness that are central to their heritage. While the Jewish people have had their share of centuries as a conquered people, they have never lost their foundations culturally that have made them unique and strong.

The Higher Dimensions

All of this dovetails into a framework, individually and community-wise, that has set a standard for living within the reality of God's nature. It is a creative path that carries the expectation of good and of higher dimensions.

Yet, the status quo is the enemy of these higher, creative dimensions in God. As Hebrews 11 sums up the exploits of the heroes of faith, it concludes with a most unusual, but insightful statement. It says that apart from us, they who have preceded us would not be made perfect. This truth works both ways, as we progressively build upon the foundations laid by previous generations.

When Solomon notes that God has put eternity in our hearts, it gives glimpse to the unspoken, insatiable quest to reach beyond the visible and to discover and apply the pieces that are lacking.

Hebrews 12 begins with the dramatic picture of the great cloud of witnesses, beyond time, surrounding us and the strong admonition to press through and not be entrapped by the encumbrances designed to seduce and hold back. Jesus said: "He who loves his life will lose it, but he who hates his life in this world will gain it." There is a place in God that far outweighs the best this world has to offer. It is in the dimensions of God beyond ourselves in which the creative and true life resides.

Moses mapped out the starting point: "All these blessings shall come upon you and overtake you, when you obey the voice of the Lord your God." (Deut 28:1) This speaks to the priority that Jesus punctuated, that you don't seek after the things of this world, you seek after God and His

Kingdom dimensions (Matt 6:33). When you seek after God, then those things we refer to as blessings will follow after us, amass and come upon us.

The creative path of discovery is one that has a parallel in embracing His glory. It explains how a member of one generation can be influenced by dimensions from their spiritual heritage in deeply penetrating something in both the natural and spiritual realms. Yet, the higher dimension that taps His power, like that of Joshua when the sun and moon stood still, resides in a foundation of knowing Him.

It is a gift drawn from His presence, of abiding in Him, which impacts the way we view things and make decisions. That gift grows from a way of thinking to an anointing that serves in developing and applying our mantle in life. In prevailing, it will transcend the natural and uncover significant matters not normally visible. It evolves as a process as the natural begins tapping the supernatural.

It is a process for all times, but especially for what lies before us. We are entering a time unlike any that has preceded us. It will be a time of progressive, higher dimensions unfolding in a single generation. It will be a time of new things with the creative on the forefront. The strategy of prayer and faith together with the strategy of community will be bedrock.

"The Spirit of the Lord rests upon me, the Spirit of wisdom and understanding, the Spirit of counsel and might, the Spirit of knowledge and the fear of the Lord." Isaiah 11:2

CHAPTER 20

SPIRITUAL CLIMATE CHANGE

"The kingdom of heaven is like a certain king who arranged a wedding for his son. But those invited made light of it and went, one to his farm, another to his business. The rest seized his servants and killed them. When the king heard, he was furious. He sent out his armies to destroy the murderers and their city. Then he said to his servants, those invited were not worthy; go into the thoroughfares of the city and as many as you find, invite to the wedding. They gathered all they found, both bad and good. So, the wedding hall was filled. When the king came in, he saw one without a wedding garment and said, 'friend, how did you come without a wedding garment?' He was speechless. Then the king commanded, 'bind him and cast him into outer darkness; where there will be weeping and gnashing of teeth.' For many are called, but few are chosen." Matthew 22:2-14

The spiritual climate defines the heart of a society. It controls the power that reigns. It has been a central target in the struggle between good and evil for ages past.

The unrighteous quest for power, masked by the perception of a utopian society, ruled by an all-knowing, supposedly "for the common good" governmental system, manifested with Hitler's Germany. At its core was the strategy of the "big lie." These were propositions laced with hope, yet so outrageous that the inclination by those under its rule, was by faith to believe them, as the communications people were subjected to were controlled by the government.

This is the same undercurrent and hope that draws adherents into radical Muslim sects. Such perverse, subtle perceptions are the foundation of the premise being presented by secular-progressive political thinkers.

Yet, this mode of thinking is only superficially political. It is spiritual.

The basis of today's world of political correctness is fast closing the gap with the world described in George Orwell's 1949 novel titled "Nineteen Eighty-Four." Orwellian "1984" terms include "Big-Brother," group-think, speak-crimes and new-speak.

It portrays a government-controlled tyranny in which power, absolute power, is sought for its own end. It is a world of omnipresent government surveillance and public manipulation.

Another "futuristic" novel of its time, published in 1931 by Aldous Huxley, "Brave New World," presents a world of pervasive psychological manipulation designed to bring the change to create a conformist, robotic-thinking society.

One of the most subtle dynamics of this premise is the removal of honor from a society's leadership. Without honor, things quickly digress into unrighteousness and lawlessness.

The opening parable in Matthew 22 uncovers the potent nature of this issue of honor. When the king announced plans for his son's wedding, pointing to the succession and his reign, it was met with rebellion and dishonor. Upon recovery, as the wedding finally was begun, those called who failed to meet the standard and respond with the honor due the spiritual significance of this event were dealt with decisively.

The Keys and the Standard

God's people, whose identities are fully in Him, hold the keys and are the key to drawing the line with this age-old conflict defining the spiritual climate. As bearers of this truth, God's people have been and are a target. If the strategy of convincing them to be like everyone else falls short, then they become objects for annihilation.

Governments are the means rather than the end. Freedom is the banner by which the Lord reigns. Honor is the underpinning of godly, true freedom.

Long ago, God established a standard within the community of His people. That standard is what we refer to as truth and the knowledge of His ways. When this standard, along with His presence are in full operation within the household of faith, then the impact of this spiritual climate on society produces positive ripples from His truth and presence.

The spiritual climate that manifests God's presence holds the potential to change everything around it. The restoration of honor is crucial to this equation.

"When the earth experiences His judgments, the inhabitants of the world learn righteousness." Isaiah 26:9

The Two Sides of Honor

The story of Job is a story of honor. Job experienced the bottom dropping out financially and health-wise. Despite his community long considering him as an honorable man, his circumstances drew accusations bringing his honor into question.

Yet, when the realities faced by Job resulted in humility and repentance that triggered a new and profound revelation of God, God honored him with an honor that far outshined that of his community.

The lynchpin that brought Job through to this new consciousness of God was that Job did not blame God. It is a factor marking the foundation of the spiritual climate in which God manifests. In all Job experienced, he upheld God's honor and as a result was conferred with an honor and a new authority that only could come from God.

The Trust Factor

Honor begets trust. In the same "two-sided" way honor is reflected in the story of Job, so the dynamic of trust operates. It is reflected by the trust conferred by man, but the trust that comes from God bears a higher level of knowing and abiding in Him and with that will engender much greater levels of authority and fruit.

"Blessed is the man who has made the Lord his trust and has not turned to the proud or to those who lapse into falsehood." Psalm 40:4

Understanding the Times

The spiritual dynamic at play in this hour has been manifesting for decades. It has involved the systematic rebranding and erosion of anything good tied to those called by His Name. It has sought to recast issues of foundational and honorable heritage. It has been a strategy of dishonor in the age-old conflict of Babylon and Chaldea.

"O God, do not remain silent and do not be still. For behold, Your enemies make an uproar, and those who hate You have exalted themselves. They make shrewd plans against Your people and conspire together against Your treasured ones. They have said, 'Come and let us wipe them out that the name of Israel be remembered no more.' For they have conspired together with one mind; against You they make a covenant." Psalm 83:1-5

Babylon and Chaldea are the chief strongholds that war against God and His people. Babylon is the spirit of the world, without the true God, empowered and propped up by Chaldea, the spirit of sorcery, the very gates of the devil's supernatural power.

The Confrontation

Still, the Bible is replete with the history of individuals and communities who would not waver in the face of death and who changed kingdoms and nations as a result. God has long reversed the bondages of evil through ones who have refused to waver before evil.

"Through you I will break nations in pieces. Through you I will destroy kingdoms and strongholds. Through you I will shatter governors and rulers. And I the Lord will repay Babylon and Chaldea." Jeremiah 51:20, 23-23

These verses in Jeremiah unveil not only the stand and the confrontational role of the household of faith against the powers-to-be in the natural, but it uncovers the source of their power, which God Himself will judge when we have done our part.

A respected prophetic voice recently commented on a word the Lord spoke to him: that revival would come when honor is restored to the fathers. Whether it is the entertainment industry or news industry, the last few decades have seen a systematic erosion of the response to the honor of any who uphold righteous values, especially targeting the role of righteous fathers.

The response begins with the household of faith. At the heart of this matter is the societal standard, how the household of faith lives in community. The honorable demonstration of the reality of God according to His standard is what the world, losing its grip on hope, longs for. It is the factor that prompts the reality of God to manifest.

"So shall they fear the name of the Lord from the west and His glory from the rising of the sun. When the enemy comes in like a flood, the Spirit of the Lord will raise up a standard against him [and put him to flight]." Isaiah 59:19 NKJV and Amplified

This manifesting consciousness of God's presence will short-circuit the masks and illusions perpetuated by evil and change the spiritual climate in its wake. At its root is the employment of power by God's people, righteous power.

Spiritual Climate Change

The spiritual climate is regulated by and governed by the role of the true intercessor and with that the culture of the community of God's people.

"Justice is turned back and righteousness stands afar off; for truth is fallen in the street and equity cannot enter. So truth fails and he who departs from evil makes himself a prey. But the LORD saw it and it displeased Him. He wondered that there was no intercessor." Isaiah 59:14-16

Numbers 25:10 describes the intentionality of intercession needed to change the spiritual climate. It tells how Phinehas, the grandson of Aaron stood in the gap and made atonement for the sin of the Israelites. His intercession was described as being zealous for God's honor. Because of that his descendents were conferred a covenant of a lasting priesthood.

The prophet Daniel stood in the gap, repenting and making atonement for the iniquity of His people. It takes the righteous to operate with this anointing and with this level of authority.

"Then Daniel turned to the Lord God and pleaded with Him in prayer and petition, with fasting and sackcloth and ashes." Daniel 9:3

Today's righteous prophetic intercessors must accept their role of standing in the gap and repenting and making supplication as Phinehas and Daniel did. In no way overlooking the potential of the role of righteous political leaders, the household of faith in the West has been guilty of putting their trust in the government for their answers while succumbing to confusion, as the anti-God forces have systematically usurped the elements of authority bearing on the spiritual climate of our society.

In the mid-1980s there was a planning conference held in Boulder, Colorado by gay activists. They mapped out a 25 year plan and proceeded to execute it. Their influence and agendas went beyond talking the talk and penetrated key circles of the media, entertainment industry, politics and even technology and business. They declared war, while the Christian community at the time was consumed with a mix of abuses of power and division – or simply found themselves confusing their role in upholding a higher standard with projecting a superficial image of being "nice people."

Spiritual climate change will not come without unequivocal confrontation.

"Paul, filled with the Holy Spirit, looked intently at the sorcerer saying, 'You who are full of all deceit and all fraud, you son of the devil, you enemy of all righteousness, will you not cease perverting the straight ways of the Lord? Now, behold, the hand of the Lord is upon you, and you shall be blind, not seeing for a time.'" Acts 13:9

The Maturity Factor

Operational maturity within the household of faith is no longer an option. For far too long we've promulgated a mind-set of being a band of followers, ever-learning and never coming to the knowledge of the truth. The great deception in this mode of thinking is that spiritual maturity is somehow tied to a higher level of doctrinal knowledge. That's the "one ups-man" approach the Pharisees gave the people. It immobilized them. Jesus came to set the people free from that trap and mobilize them. True spiritual maturity is putting your faith in action, being doers of the Word and not hearers only, who deceive themselves (James 1:22).

Elijah risked it all to face overwhelming odds arrayed against him in order to confront evil and uphold God's honor. All it takes is a righteous remnant with the faith and courage to risk everything.

"Have you entered the treasury of snow, or have you seen the storehouse of hail, which I have reserved for the time of trouble, for the day of battle and war?" Job 38:22, 23

The wedding feast is fast approaching, which will distinguish those who will be the chosen from those called.

The heroes of faith spoken of in the book of Hebrews were not seduced by their comforts or their quest to maintain their survival. They conformed to the truth spoken of by Jesus that the greatest love (John 15:13) is that evidenced by those willing to give up their lives for God's honor and for those who would follow them. Some did just that. Others, in facing the crucible, walked into spectacular miracles.

Such a resolute mind-set is the maturity factor needed to trigger His glory and change the spiritual climate. God's glory will not abide with the glory sought by men.

The ground occupied by those willing to sacrifice at the level Jesus pointed to is sacred ground. God is not looking for glory-hounds, but rather the Stephens and those with the spirit and spiritual maturity to confront the realities and uphold God's honor with their all.

"The LORD said to Moses, 'Phinehas, son of Eleazar, the son of Aaron, the priest, has turned my anger away from the Israelites; for he was as zealous as I am for my honor among them, so that in my zeal I did not put an end to them. Therefore tell him I am making my covenant of peace with him. He and his descendants will have a covenant of a lasting priesthood, because he was zealous for the honor of his God and made atonement for the Israelites.'" Numbers 25:10-13

CHAPTER 21

WHEN HONOR IS RESTORED

"But for you who fear My name, the sun of righteousness will rise with healing in its wings; and you will go forth and skip about like calves from the stall. In that day, He will restore the hearts of the fathers to their children and the hearts of the children to their fathers, so that I will not come and smite the land with a curse." Malachi 4: 2, 6

These are times of restoration. Isaiah wrote that there would come a time when darkness would cover the earth and deep darkness the peoples. Yet, these would be the times in which the Lord begins to dramatically restore His order, as the Glory of the Lord comes upon His people, those walking in the fear of the Lord.

Ezekiel foresaw such a time when every vision would be fulfilled without delay. (Ezek 12:23)

Malachi's prophecy similarly points to restoration in the face of great reprobation, a depravity which impacts even the household of faith. The opening scripture is in the context of a day of judgment, but also a day of preparation that restores key elements to the foundations established for God's people.

At the crux of the elements restored, that bring the turnaround, is honor.

The Dynamic of Honor

What we refer to as "knowing" the Lord is a progressive thing. The life of Abraham illustrates this truth. It is a process that takes place over a lifetime. Even for those like Abraham who keep their hand to the plow, the depths of knowing Him are such that there is always more.

Central to knowing Him is the factor of honor. The book of Hebrews reveals that we cannot take this true honor to ourselves, but rather it is granted only by God. Job, an honorable man by his own accomplishments went through a major life-transition to find that when, stripped of the things this life was able to offer, he was able to see God for the magnitude of Who He truly is. When that happened, God bestowed an honor upon Job that far outweighed Job's previous honor.

It only takes a glimmer of His presence.

The honor bestowed by God changes everything. Jesus spent His earthly ministry conveying the dynamics tied to honoring the Father and the secrets to abiding in His presence. From that honor and abiding we begin to grasp the principles Jesus imparted on how the Kingdom of God operates, of how we employ righteous power in a corrupt world.

"For the Father judges no one, but has given all judgment to the Son, that all should honor the Son just as they honor the Father." John 5:21-23

The Sphere

We have some friends who God called to the mission field. The area of their calling is extremely hard ground spiritually. Their first two years were grueling and exhausting. They were filled with what seemed as constant reversals and steep, uphill challenges.

"Many will be offended, betray one another and hate one another. False prophets will rise up and deceive many. Because lawlessness will abound, the love of many will grow cold." Matthew 24: 10-12

Yet they persisted in upholding the fear of the Lord. They never fell short in praying, which they sometimes did just to survive. They likewise never gave up.

Then they were invited to minister in a distant province from where they had been sent. The difference was startling and dramatic. This province was one of two in this nation known to be populated with Christians. They ministered in the same way as they did where they were plowing new ground, but instead miracles took place at every turn. It provided the impetus to return to their assignment and expect more largely from the result of the anointing and authority the time of refreshing confirmed that they still wielded.

Many are those called to plow new ground. So it is with the hard ground of the times we have entered.

Paul wrote that to each is given a sphere or a boundary in which to operate. It is a boundary of authority, a sphere of influence. Within that sphere we have the potential of great power as agents of change. That change when employed according to the Kingdom model and not a religious model will impact the culture, as well as the economy and the power structures of that sphere.

Yet, there are places where the forces of darkness are so entrenched that it takes time for the change to take root. It will. It requires establishing the fear of God.

"Your words have been arrogant against Me, says the LORD. You have said, 'It is vain to serve God; and what profit is it that we have kept His charge, and that we have walked in mourning [repentance] before the LORD of hosts?'" Malachi 3: 13-14

Establishing the fear of God involves upholding the magnitude of God's honor. It is not about us, but Him. When we get it reversed, we broach the realm of making an idol out of our ministry and the anointing given to pave the way for our calling. Jesus outlined the principles by which we would not be ensnared by this deception.

They are the principles of the Kingdom. Most are paradoxes to the way the world thinks and employs power. We live by dying. We gain by giving. We bless those who curse us. Wisdom comes from simplicity. Humility is a protective armor. We lead by serving. Honor comes from humility. The principles of the Kingdom are the keys to employing His power in unrighteous settings.

A Warrior's Honor

Throughout the Word of God, reference is given to military people. Those who have repeatedly faced life and death battles hold to a code of honor. They are ones who recognize one another quickly and just as quickly differentiate the phonies, the braggarts and the glory-hounds. They understand the serious risks of employing great power.

Jesus was amazed in His encounter with the Centurion who drew the parallel between his authority and how faith operates. God saw Cyrus long before his birth and relished in what He would do through Cyrus on behalf of His people Israel.

What is it about the warrior's honor? They understand authority. They are people of faith and strategy. They understand how to steward power. They are people of discipline. They respond to duty and know how to operate in unity. They are calculated risk-takers and people of action. They are willing to sacrifice for a cause. They have a willingness to die for what they believe in. They lead by serving.

Honor is at the core of the warrior's life-tenets, the warrior's way of thinking.

Understanding that we are agents of change requires a grasp of the honor of the warrior. Stewards of God's power must grasp and embrace this level of honor.

The Snare of the King's Tantrum

Agents of change embracing the code of the warrior understand the importance of the big-picture and the long-term.

The story of Hezekiah is a story of the long-term being sacrificed for the short-term. Hezekiah was a righteous king. During his life there had been exploits as he had honored the Lord in the way he ruled Judah. His standoff against Sennacherib king of Syria (2 Kings 19:36) was striking. He restored the temple worship and Passover (2 Chron 29:20, 30:1) Yet, in his final days, he fell short in embracing the honor of the warrior.

Responding in a tantrum of bitterness when the prophet told him his days were concluding, Scripture says after being healed, Hezekiah became proud. In his final days, Isaiah rebuked his spiritual short-sightedness and prophesied the impact of his actions on future generations (2 Kings 20:14).

Restoring the Generation Link

Among the mysteries in God's Word is the link between generations. The restoration of the honor – bestowed by God – must begin with the restoration of honor within the community of God's people. It is the glue that will bring the unity and maturity Paul explained to the Ephesians. It is the catalyst in rebuilding the broken walls in the eroded values of our society.

"You will rebuild the ancient ruins and will raise up the foundations of many generations. You will be called the repairer of the breach, the restorer of the streets in which to dwell." Isaiah 58:12

Honor restored is what Malachi prophesied in terms of the hearts of the children being restored to the fathers so that the land would not be smitten with a curse.

It is what Gabriel told Zacharias of his coming son John who would operate in the spirit and power of Elijah, to make ready a people prepared for the Lord. The honor that links the generations releases an exponential power within the community of God's people. It is the reason for the importance given to the father's blessing in the days of the Patriarchs. When the generations link together, then unity will come.

One of the facets of the spiritual turmoil of the 1960s was the cultural war against authority and honor. Duty was ridiculed. The media has long mocked the authority of the fathers, in their scorn of shows such as "Leave It to Beaver." Honor was the bulls-eye in the undermining of the accepted righteous values of that day.

When honor is in evidence, it draws the attention of the Lord, as in Jesus' response to the Centurion and God's calling of Cyrus. Abraham was a man of honor, which attracted the presence of the Lord. It was the honor of the warrior in Daniel in the face of adversity that brought angelic intervention.

"The angel touched me and strengthened me and said, "O man greatly beloved, fear not! Peace be to you; be strong, yes, be strong!" When he spoke I was strengthened and said, "Let my lord speak for you have strengthened me." Daniel 10: 18-19

It was the honor that emerged in the face of calamity when jailed (Acts 12:7), when Peter's heart had finally became undivided, that brought the angel to free him.

The Righteous Remnant

When that level of honor is restored merely a remnant in the household of faith is all it will take to release the turning. When the hearts of the children once again can adhere to the authority of the fathers, with the honor of the warrior being restored to the fathers, it will mark the turning of the restoration of all things.

Honor and authority, God's authority, are linked. God's honor in the face of tribulation actuates an authority that will change the spiritual climate of a nation.

"He who speaks from himself seeks his own glory; but He who seeks the glory of the One who sent Him is true, and no unrighteousness is in Him." John 7:18-19

Many are called, but few are chosen. It is an hour in which even the elect are subject to being deceived. Yet, those who prevail will be given a mantle of fire, an authority that dispels darkness and brings the disruptive spiritual change that opens the gates to His presence.

Jesus indicated that His message of abiding would bring great joy. From that would come the heart of the warrior that would love as Jesus loved and be willing to lay down their lives for their friends. Peter once bragged that he would be of that heart, but braggadocio fails. He did. Similarly, when he tried to respond in his own strength in the Garden of Gethsemane with a sword, he again failed.

Peter had to get past himself. For Peter to assume the mantle of fire and authority that he was called to operate with took a level of humility and honor that accompanies the heart of a seasoned and tested warrior.

There is a righteous remnant that has been prepared. These are ones who have been tested, who have emerged from the fires without the smell of smoke. It is why humility and honor are the brand-marks of true warriors. It is these who will be the catalysts for revival who will wield the mantle of fire that brings the change and restoration being orchestrated by God in this hour.

"I came to send fire on the earth and how I wish it were already kindled. But I have a baptism to be baptized with and how distressed I am until it is accomplished." Luke 12:49-50

"Bless the Lord all you His angels, who excel in strength doing His Word, heeding the voice of His Word. Bless the Lord all you His hosts, you ministers of His doing His pleasure. Bless the Lord all you His works in all places of His dominion. Bless the Lord O my soul." Psalm 103: 20-22

CHAPTER 22

GLORY MANIFESTED

"The glory which You gave Me I have given them, that they may be one just as We are one: I in them, and You in Me; that they may be made perfect in one." John 17:22-23

This segment of Jesus' high priestly prayer taps a very key aspect of walking out a call of God: abiding in Him.

While some conclude from these verses to make unity the goal, unity is not the goal, but rather the fruit. Unity will be the fruit of abiding. It likewise is not a conformity type of unity, but rather being so in-sync with the Lord and His heart, that those truly abiding in Him will simply be on the same page within the individuality of their spheres and callings.

"In that day you will know that I am in My Father and you in me and I in you." John 14:19

As a young disciple, one of my two primary mentors shared about a time when he was a part of a camp meeting retreat. As those attending the gathering sought the Lord, he recounted how there came a tangible consciousness of God's presence. As they continued seeking Him, he described something as like a smoke that descended on them which brought an even greater awareness of God's presence.

For three days, this holy presence was so strong that the only thing anyone wanted was to bask in His presence. What had been scheduled, comparatively, no longer had any significance.

"The temple was filled with smoke from the glory of God and from His power, and no one was able to enter." Revelation 15:8

What took place was a manifestation of God's glory, triggered by hungry hearts, in unison, from steadfastly seeking Him. The need is to bring this consciousness of His presence into our everyday lives.

The influence of this mentor's passion resonated deeply with us, as my wife and I had come to faith as a result of a very real and insatiable spiritual hunger that pervaded our workplaces and neighborhoods. It was during the early days of the charismatic revival.

Everyone was talking about Jesus and the Holy Spirit. People would spontaneously gather together just to pray and seek God. Those affected were acutely aware of what they were hearing from God. The miraculous became commonplace. Many experienced dramatic and life-changing answers to prayer. It was a time of abandoning yourself to God. Nothing carried any greater priority.

"The house of the LORD was filled with a cloud, so that the priests could not stand to minister because of the cloud, for the glory of the LORD filled the house of God." 2 Chronicles 5:13-14

This verse describes a time when the glory manifested and was imparted, as in John 17 Jesus imparted the glory He had received to His disciples. Such times trigger God-directed change and the restoration of truths and mysteries that have been squeezed out by the cares of life and the religious precepts of men.

Abiding in Him overcomes the seductions of worldly cares and the precepts of men. Abiding in Him and being stewards of His glory carries a cost with parameters that open the path into the supernatural, into the realm of angels and His presence.

The Parameters

Jesus warned that wielding this power would not only impact the spiritual climate, but would bring tribulation. David understood this.

"Many are they who say of me, "There is no help for him in God." But You, O Lord, are a shield for me, my glory and the One who lifts up my head." Psalm 3:3

Becoming the source of changing the spiritual climate requires more than zeal to weather the opposition and backlash, which can, in the natural, make progress seem impossible. Yet, that is just the point. With God, in Him all things are possible. The pathway in which His glory manifests was described by Jesus as narrow and difficult.

This pathway is the foundation for the mandate for change and restoration for this hour. It requires consistent spiritual maintenance, the continual renewal of our mind-sets, operating beyond ourselves, producing fruit that abides and tapping the generational bridges.

Spiritual Maintenance. Abiding is a lifetime process. Spiritual maintenance of personal prayer and a consistent washing of God's Word must be an ongoing priority. It requires discipline and it requires sacrifice.

Personal maintenance will be found to be progressive, with its intensity directly linked to one's spiritual maturity. One's spiritual maturity will be demonstrated by the fruit. The fruit will be evidenced by the level of change being wielded by the mantle.

Regular, personal, quality time with the Lord must be given priority. Jesus spent entire nights alone in prayer. Many stress the importance of a well-organized prayer-shield. I don't disagree. However, the Lord once let me know that regardless of the number of prayers I mobilize through others, that my exploits would never exceed the level represented by my own prayers. A prayer-shield serves to augment this baseline.

Renewed Mind-Sets. Consistent time with the Lord influences our thinking. We need our thinking and attitudes constantly renewed and aligned according to God's heart and priorities. Our thinking determines how we believe and how we act in faith.

Mind-sets go deep. While they include our attitudes, which are the determinants of our behavior, they go beyond our attitudes. They also include the often very subtle cultural predispositions that the Bible refers to as iniquities. The input from the world pollutes our thinking and cultural tendencies,

True people of faith do not conform to the world's way of thinking or doing. One of the biggest challenges God's people have faced over the centuries has been the lure to be like everyone else, to be accepted. One of the first premises of leadership is that real leadership can never be achieved through acceptance or being liked. Leadership has its foundations in honor, trust and respect.

Our identities in God are distinctive. We are called to be leaders, each within our own spheres. The Word of God tells us that we have been chosen to demonstrate God's reality. That's the first order of things. It requires mind-sets aligned with God's. That forms the basis of one's calling in God.

Beyond Ourselves. In the final analysis, it is not about us. That's why we need our mind-sets continually being renewed. Piercing the veil beyond self is the place Jesus sought for His disciples. For Peter, it took a final word from the Lord after Jesus' resurrection for Peter to begin walking in that place that the Lord saw in Peter when He first met him and discerned His destiny.

Years ago, during a time alone seeking the Lord, the Lord told me: "Morris, you're too introspective." What the Lord was telling me had nothing to do with getting our attitudes in line with His truth and priorities. Instead it gave focus to a Western mantra of self-improvement that goes beyond this level of alignment. Being too introspective can become a fine-line distraction and illusion that distorts the balance of our callings. Walking out a call of God requires humility.

Humility is the recognition that we can't, but He can. Humility is a constant dependence on Him. Humility is the realization that a significant part of the "cleanup" is God's prevue and our response needs to faithfully hold fast to Him, seeking Him and being "doers of the Word." It's learning to walk with God with a purity of heart that is beyond ourselves.

Business people tend to be doers. For those with callings like Joseph and Daniel and Peter, it means piercing the veil and flowing in a place beyond our human capabilities. It's not what we can do for God, but rather what we allow the Lord to do through us. That's the essence of the greater sacrificial love that Jesus modeled.

Fruit that Abides. Jesus made it very clear that we would be known, not by our activity, but by the fruits from our activity.

Bearing fruit is a strong part of Jesus' message. It is the result of flowing in the Spirit according to our gifts. Bearing fruit that remains transfers the anointing and calling to those being ministered to.

The glory will come when we are abiding and consistently finding our life-source in Him. Bearing fruit that abides will come from our lives operating in that place beyond ourselves, in Him.

"If you abide in Me and my words abide in you, you will ask what you will and it will be done for you." John 15:7

The Generational Bridge. Among the mysteries being restored in this day is the generational bridge. The generational bridge is more than mentoring and passing the baton to the next generation, although that is certainly an important part. The generational bridge involves mantles, the callings that transcend that of an individual and are sparked and fulfilled through generational bridges.

Joseph the Patriarch was the fourth generation from His great-grandfather Abraham. From the promises and mantle given to His great-grandfather, Joseph not only brought an incredible fullness to this mantle, but he set the stage for what would be the next generational bridge, the alignment of which would be actuated by Moses.

We have reached a time in which there has come a convergence that is beyond the current generation. We catch a glimmer of this convergence from the description in Hebrews of the great cloud of witnesses.

It is a time when not only do generations pave the way for one another, but there is an added dimension where anointed members of connecting generations are working together and bringing a dimension seldom seen operating in days past. In short, it is a time when the anointings of Abrahams, Isaacs and Jacobs begin operating together and sparking new dimensions. As we abide in Him and apply the parameters of this pathway, these connected anointings will serve as three-fold cords that trigger supernatural change and restoration.

The Mandate for Change and Restoration

Jesus came to raise the standard. He raised the bar. He reset the spiritual default to conform to God's heart and priorities. Resetting priorities in this way releases the mantle of fire of God's glory to bring change and restoration.

"He who speaks from himself seeks his own glory; but He who seeks the glory of the One who sent Him is true, and no unrighteousness is in Him." John 7:18

With the glory Jesus imparted to His followers came the authority to reestablish God's order in the midst of a world masked and ruled by disorder.

"I came to bring fire to the earth and how I wish it were already kindled, but I have a baptism to be baptized with and how distressed I am until it is accomplished." Luke 12:49-50

The fire that Jesus had kindled manifested significantly following the outpouring of the Holy Spirit. It was and is the mantle of fire. Scripture describes it as a time when great fear (of God) came upon all the church and to as many who were exposed to and were hearing about the supernatural manifestations happening. It was a time marked by the consciousness of His presence in everyday life.

Simultaneously, it was a time of great spiritual backlash. Stephen and John's brother James were martyred. Peter was imprisoned, yet was supernaturally delivered as the saints faithfully prayed. Angelic manifestations and miracles were common.

"Now the angel of the Lord stood by him and a light shown in the prison and the chains fell off his hands. Then the angel said to him, follow me. So he followed him, but did not know that what the angel was doing was real. When they were past the first and second guard posts they came to the iron gate that leads to the city, which opened of its own accord and immediately the angel departed from him." Acts 12: 7-10

Change and amazing things will result when God's glory manifests. It incorporates the power that defeated death and the grave. It brings change that aligns and restores God's ancient truths and covenants with Abraham, Moses and David.

"Thus says the Lord: Stand at the crossroads and look. Then ask for the ancient paths where the good way lies. Then walk in it and you will find rest for your souls." Jeremiah 6:16

Getting the abiding factor and priorities right sets the stage for the glory to manifest. It is the foundation for the authority needed to bring change and restoration.

"The words that I speak to you I do not speak on My own authority; but the Father who dwells in Me does the works." John 14:10

It is the fine line of our walk with Him for this hour.

"So, open the gates, so that all who are righteous may enter, those who have remained faithful. The steadfast of mind You will keep in perfect peace, because he trusts in You. For in You we have an everlasting Rock. The way of the righteous is level and smooth. O Upright One, make the

path of the righteous straight. While following the way of your judgments, we have eagerly waited for You. At night my soul longs for You. Indeed my spirit seeks you diligently. For when the earth experiences Your judgments, the inhabitants of the world learn righteousness." Isaiah 26:2-3, 7-10

AFTERWARD

EMPOWERMENT AND RESTORATION

"Therefore, hear the word of the LORD, you scoffers, who rule this people, because you have said, "We have made a covenant with death, and with Sheol we have made a pact. The overwhelming scourge will not reach us when it passes by for we have made falsehood our refuge and we have concealed ourselves with deception." Isaiah 28:14-15

False images and illusions permeate the portrayal of developments in today's world.

From the beginning, the people of God have been the standard bearers. When mobilized and trained, God's people will have reached a point to be deployed. Before any deployment there will be operation orders. From the operation orders the leaders being deployed develop strategy.

Yet before there can be a sound strategy, precision discernment is needed to discern the battle lines. Understanding the enemy and the alternatives of what can be expected is critical.

The enemy's strategy is falsehood and concealment. Its highest order of design is to keep us from the place of deployment. So, in approaching operational deployment, the planning to maximize our strategy must begin by identifying and removing entanglements embedded deep within the Body. The mission begins by exposing and canceling the covenant with death.

Some have observed that to a certain degree the reversals happening in the world today reverberate what has been operationally hidden and sometimes not so hidden within the Body. With the level of pollution that has found its way within the Church over the centuries, wisdom shouts the need to clean out the defilements before deploying. While some have reduced the issue to one of character and flesh, it entails more and taps the maturity and training necessary for a martial mobilization.

In other words, before the Body can deal with significant spiritual issues impacting the world with more than fragmented deployments, it needs to get cleaned up and properly prepared.

"He will send out His angels and gather out of His Kingdom all things that offend and those who practice lawlessness." Matthew 13:41

The prophet Isaiah saw past the illusions and false images in the camp of God's people and called it for what it was: an alliance with death. In short, Isaiah was saying that in playing it safe, in trying to be like everyone else and using a playbook guided by the world's standard, the rulers in Jerusalem had stubbornly made a pact with the devil.

Many leaders within the Body today are in over their heads. Many are missing the mark and trying to compensate by gravitating to the peripheries defined by pop-Christian culture. The Apostle Paul described the dynamic as having zeal without knowledge. The masks are being removed and the balance of Spirit and Truth is being restored.

When the response is shaped by anything short of biblical foundations and a truly humble dependence on the Spirit of the Lord, be it the precepts of men or the approval of men, we have entered a time in which the results will be catastrophic.

Authority to Meet the Challenge

It is an issue of having the authority and focus to meet the challenge. The misguided leadership styles of modern-day Ahabs, acquiescing to domineering, power-mongering Jezebels will either draw the line or have their mantles removed.

Those whose exploits have been based on weak foundations and bluster, together with a touch of grace need to make the transition. The authority for the challenge has a cost. That cost was described by John the Baptist that: "He (Jesus) must increase and we must decrease." The Kingdom cost of authority begins with a fresh and potent dose of humility.

Despite illusions to the contrary, there is no single segment of the Body with sufficient grasp of the big-picture needed to deploy. Isaiah had strong words to say about those with their fingers pointed in scorn (Isaiah 58), who themselves failed to measure according to their own standard.

We need one another and the unique spiritual capabilities given to the various parts of the Body. It is the time in which every joint is needed to be fitted to the place of their purpose in preparing for deployment. That will take humility, wisdom and the leading of the Spirit. Segments in the Body depending solely on their own uniqueness or elitism will be at best vulnerable to the seductive encounters with the covenant of death.

Deployment will mark a time of restoration of the foundations of the ancient paths.

"Thus says the Lord: Stand at the crossroads and look. Then ask for the ancient paths, where the good way lies. Then walk in it and you will find rest for your souls." Jeremiah 6:16

Restoring the Ancient Paths

The Lord is restoring the biblical foundations of our faith that have been masked and replaced with paganistic precepts of men. From the days of the early Church the battle lines were fiercely deployed around issues empowering the Body, matters that kept its efforts connected to the power and flow of the Spirit.

Systematically, the power of the Spirit once ascribed to the early church has been replaced by an anemic institutional power that has resulted in a church history rife in corruption, politics and pride. Even today, the precepts that encourage a weak institution rather than a vibrant Spirit-led organism that changes cultures are only exceeded by those who ridicule people of faith who have sought to emulate the power of the early church, only to fall. The deception is in treating the reach as sin rather than the fall.

The glory that has consistently manifested from the days of the patri-archs is being restored. From the forgotten covenants, to the foundations laid out by Moses, to the tabernacle of David, all significant elements of the vibrant dynamic of the early church, are being rediscovered and restored.

God's means of making His people the head and not the tail have from the start included the provision needed to compensate for the Chaldeans, Jihadists and alliances of sorceries that have amassed in a fallen world. As the Church increasingly sheds its non-biblical practices and blind-spots to get reacquainted with its biblical Hebrew roots, the times call for a re-embracing of the biblical feast-days and days of rest that the Lord set aside to corporately empower and align His people spiritually.

The Lord has always provided the means by which His people can avoid the spiritual ambushes and backlash created by the frenetic machi-nations of God's enemies. The doctrinal sacred cows with no foundations in Scripture that leave us unprotected are being scrutinized as the church restores its biblical foundations.

Regaining the Maturity Standard

Scripture outlines a sequence of Christian maturity. Beginning with being a follower, one progresses to become a disciple, then a servant. Servants graduate to become friends, with the design of them finally becoming the sons that Paul described to the Romans.

"For creation eagerly awaits the revealing of the sons of God . . . . . that it might be delivered from the bondage of corruption." Romans 8:19, 21

Rick Joyner has commented that 90 percent of the Body in the West is stuck between the untrained and unprepared follower and the disciple stages.

Vital to the maturity standard needed for deployment is the recognition of the operational big-picture and the myopia that results from elitism. Like true Kingdom authority the cost is humility and an awareness of the reality of the roles of the various parts fitted together to accomplish the big-picture, grand-strategy.

It is also an issue of commitment and sacrifice. Jesus admonished us to embrace this level of commitment and sacrifice, one that is willing to give your life for your friends (John 15:13). Veterans of real combat understand this. Commitment and sacrifice underscore Communist ideology in their zeal for a Communistic world. In the early 1940s, as a convert to Christianity from being editor of London's Communist tabloid, "The Daily Worker," Douglas Hyde was disillusioned by the lack of commitment he found in the church ("Dedication and Leadership," 1992, Notre Dame Press).

Yet, before us are days that will separate the tares from the wheat, during which the truly committed among the brethren will shine like the brightness of the sky.

The Empowerment of the Josephs

"Let the blessing come on the head of Joseph, and on the crown of the head of him who was separated from his brothers. His glory is like a first-born bull. Together with them he shall push the peoples to the ends of the earth; they are the ten thousands of Ephraim, and they are the thousands of Manasseh." Deuteronomy 33:13-17

The Josephs are those among the "first-born," apostolic-prophetic, forerunner-leaders who have submitted to the maturity process and have been prepared as friends and sons. They wield the authority to restore and with promotions orchestrated solely by the Spirit, they will establish redemptive alliances with modern-day Pharaohs and Cyruses.

They will be the challenge to the scoffers, the rulers who have made a covenant with death. They are the forerunners who will be in position to mobilize those willing to humble and yield themselves to the most rigorous training and are willing to face the highest risks in deployment. Within the military are those who play it safe with desk-jobs, who map out safe careers that keep them out of the perils of battle.

However, then there are those who operate beyond the political games with the hearts of seasoned lions who are willing to face the realities and costs of the battle. These are those who will wield the authority that changes the course of nations.

The Restoring of Israel

"Yet the Lord will lift up a standard for the nations, and assemble the banished ones of Israel, and gather the dispersed of Judah from the corners of the earth. Then the jealousy of Ephraim will depart, and those who harass Judah will be cut off." Isaiah 11:12-13

Israel is the pivot point in this drama. Not only is it targeted as the enemy seeks to fuel the alliance with death, it is the flashpoint for the battle globally. It is the prize from which the promises to Abraham and his descendents will be gleaned by the great cloud of witnesses (Heb 12:1) who have paved the way before us, along with those in this hour who prove themselves as faithful friends and sons.

With the authority, along with the restoration of the ancient paths, the maturity standard and deployment of the Josephs will emerge an alignment that breaks the power of the covenant of death. It will be a demonstration of the Lord's judgment as we prepare and deploy.

"Behold, I lay in Zion a stone for a foundation, a tried stone, a precious cornerstone, a sure foundation. Whoever believes will not act hastily. I will make justice the measuring line, and righteousness the plumb line. The hail will sweep away the refuge of lies, and the waters will overflow the hiding place. The covenant with death will be annulled, and the agreement with Sheol will not stand." Isaiah 28:16-18

Isaiah 60 portrays an intense time of turmoil and change. Isaiah 60 has begun to be played out in this day. It describes the spiritual battle ground as the Lord releases His order into His creation and brings the restoration to fulfill the promises He has long ago extended to His faithful ones.

"Arise, shine, for your light has come and the glory of the LORD has risen upon you. For behold, darkness will cover the earth and deep darkness the peoples. But the LORD will rise upon you and His glory will appear upon you. Nations will come to your light and kings to the brightness of your rising." Isaiah 60:1-3

As the Body sheds its paganistic illusions and once again embraces its position of power, it will be deployed as one. With the mantle of fire, its light and power will shatter the darkness and restore not just ancient truths, but become the critical mass toward releasing the power that actuates the fulfillment of the resurrection in making all things new for the age being birthed.

"Go through, go through the gates, clear the way for the people; build up, build up the highway, remove the stones, lift up a standard over the peoples. Behold, the LORD has proclaimed to the end of the earth, say to the daughter of Zion, "Lo, your salvation comes; behold His reward is with Him, and His recompense before Him." And they will call them, "The holy people, the redeemed of the LORD"; and you will be called, "Sought out, a city not forsaken." Isaiah 62:10-12

APPENDIX

PRAYER FOR HEARING GOD MORE CLEARLY

*L*ord God, in the Name of Jesus, I come boldly before your throne. Cleanse my heart O God. Thank You that I am cleansed by the blood of Jesus and I have invited the Holy Spirit to live within me. I bring every thought of my mind and every impression in my heart into captivity to the obedience of Jesus. Lord, I want to hear what You have to say. I trust You to communicate to me.

And in the Name of Jesus, I take authority over every fleshly strong-hold along with every demonic and interfering spirit. I forbid any enemy activity to operate in my mind or soul. I open my heart to the Holy Spirit – to inspire, to guide, to illuminate and reveal to me truth, insights and perspectives that will anoint my efforts in all You have before me.

I take authority over fear, anxiety, doubt and unbelief in the name of Jesus. I bind any negative, critical or condemning spirits in the Name of Jesus and forbid you to interfere with or in any way to imitate God's voice to me.

Lord, I thank you for being in charge of every aspect of my being and for all that will unfold in this process. I look forward to growing in this new dimension with you and for what You have planned for me through it. In the Name of Jesus. Amen.

APPENDIX

PLANNING ELEMENTS TO MENTOR EMERGING LEADERS

- **The Natural Gifts**
- **The Spiritual Gifts**
- **The Dream . . .in Serving Others**
- **The Gateways of Opportunity**
- **The Vision as a Community Builder**
- **Those Being Served**
- **The Mentors**
- **The Goals for Five Years from Now**
- **Strategies for the Community Good**

AUTHOR

MORRIS E. RUDDICK

E ntrepreneur, consultant, minister and business owner, Morris Ruddick has led development of entrepreneurial activities in critical needy areas and brought together combined business-ministry initiatives in several nations, with a focus on assisting believers in lands of persecution and distress. Mr. Ruddick's Kingdom agendas reflect a unique merging of the secular and the spiritual with initiatives based on biblical principles of business. Since 1995, he has been at the forefront of encouraging and mobilizing spiritually-minded business leaders to step out in faith by combining their entrepreneurial and spiritual gifts to build communities and impact their nations.

Mr. Ruddick's Kingdom agendas have spanned five continents with hands-on activities in Russia, Belarus, Nigeria, Ethiopia, Botswana, South Africa, Italy, India, Afghanistan, China, Vietnam and Israel. His Kingdom business initiatives have included entrepreneurial startup programs, training for spiritual business leaders and community building strategies for lands of persecution and oppression. His programs are based on biblical and Jewish models of business which draw on God's creativity even during times of change.

He helped organize and launch, and continues serving as board member for the Joseph Project, an Israeli-based international consortium of humanitarian aid that assists Israeli immigrants and citizens. Israel's Technology Incubator Program is listed among the clients he has served. He is a former board member of the Nehemiah Fund, an Israeli non-profit (amuta) that has provided grants to members of Israel's believing community facing economic distress.

He spent 19 years on the board of Marilyn Hickey Ministries and Orchard Road Christian Center where he was Chairman of both the

Compensation and Audit Committees. He is a member of the Messianic Jewish Alliance. He served as Corporate Secretary of the International Christian Chamber of Commerce-USA and is a board member of Love Botswana Outreach. His activities also include being board advisor to the Kingdom Chamber of Commerce for Africa. In addition to His seminars on doing business God's way, he has been a national speaker for a range of gatherings ranging from the National Religious Broadcasters, Mike and Cindy Jacob's Out of the Box Marketplace Conferences, the GCOWE Missions Conference, Os Hillman's Marketplace Ministry Leader's Summit, Peter Wagner's Roundtable on Kingdom Wealth and the Kingdom Economic Yearly Summit (KEYS).

Over the years, he has served executive suite management with his planning and strategy development talents in a diversity of progressive mid-sized operations, ministry groups, and Fortune 500 companies. He has been at the helm of designing and implementing two successful corporate turnarounds, one being for a $1.4 billion firm.

His time as a US Marine Corps officer during the height of the Vietnam conflict included leading both infantry and recon units, as well as serving as a senior battalion advisor with the Vietnamese Marine Corps. He headed up the mobile training team/program that prepared parachute-scuba qualified Marines (Force Recon) for reconnaissance and special operations. Mr. Ruddick was awarded the Silver Star, two Bronze Stars, the Navy Commendation Medal and the Vietnamese Medal of Honor for his actions in combat.

He holds ordination papers from the United Christian Ministerial Association, a BS from Northwestern University; and an MS in communications and doctoral work in statistics from Oklahoma State University; as well as a year of biblical studies at Oral Roberts University.

CONTACT INFORMATION

To contact the author
to speak at your conference of marketplace leaders
or gathering of supporters of the persecuted church
please write

Morris Ruddick
Global Initiatives Foundation
P.O. Box 370291
Denver, CO 80237 USA

or email:

info@strategic-initiatives.org

or call 303.741-9000 and leave a message

You may wish to visit the Global Initiatives Foundation website.
It contains additional information.
The website address is:

http://www.strategic-initiatives.org

The Strategic Intercession Global Network (SIGN)
contains additional articles:

www.strategicintercession.org

CPSIA information can be obtained
at www.ICGtesting.com
Printed in the USA
FSOW01n0530010216
16363FS